Where the Angolans are Playing Football

LANDEG WHITE was born in south Wales and has taught in Trinidad, Malawi, Sierra Leone, Zambia, and England. Among his various books are studies of V.S. Naipaul, of Mozambican and Malawian history, and of southern African praise poetry, together with five collections of poems. His translation of Camões' *The Lusíads* won the Texeira Gomes prize for 1998. He is married with two sons, and lives in Carapinheira, Portugal where he teaches at the Universidade Aberta (Open University). His website is accessible at www.landegwhite.com.

T0163077

Where the Angolans are Playing Football

Selected and New Poems

Landeg White

Parthian
The Old Surgery
Napier Street
Cardigan
SA43 1ED
www.parthianbooks.co.uk

First published in 2003

ISBN 1-902638-30-1

Typeset in Sabon

Printed and bound by Dinefwr Press, Llandybie

With Support from the Parthian Collective

Parthian is an independent publisher that works with the support
of the Arts Council of Wales and the Welsh Books Council

British Library Cataloguing in Publication Data.
A cataloguing record for this book is available from the British
Library.

Cover Design: Marc Jennings

For Alice of course,
but for Martin & John too,
and their namesakes.

Acknowledgements

Acknowledgements are due to the editors of *The Independent*, *Kunapipi*, *Mau* (Malawi), *Moving Worlds*, *Odi* (Malawi), *Poetry Review*, *Poetry Wales*, *Southern African Review of Books*, *Stand*, *Thames Poetry*, the *Times Literary Supplement*, the *1985 Anthology of the Arvon Poetry Competition*, and *A Talent(ed) Digger* (ed. Maes-Jelinek, Collier & Davis, 1996), where some of these poems first appeared. 'Bacalhau', 'The Three Graces' and 'October's Sickle Moon' were first published in Portuguese in *Superfícies e Interiores: Poemas de Landeg White* (Introdução, Selecção, Tradução e Notas de Hélio Osvaldo Alves, CEMAR 1995).

For Captain Stedman: Poems was published by Harry Chambers/Peterloo Poets (1983), *The View from the Stockade* and *Bounty* by Dangaroo Press (1991 and 1993), and *South* and *Travellers Palm* by CEMAR (Figueira da Foz, Portugal, 1999 and 2001).

Contents

From *Bounty* (1993)

From *South* (1999)

From *Traveller's Palm* (2002)

New Poems

From
For Captain Stedman
(1983)

Afternoons, Mozambique

Senhor Santos is forty-four.
He came with the army and stayed on;
now he owns a store,

a corrugated iron
roof and pink bulging walls
with Santos in vermilion.

From time to time he sells
dried fish, cokes,
a piece of cloth, olive oil.

The floor is cluttered with flour sacks
and boxes of sardines.
The trapped heat is like smoke.

Every windless afternoon
he sleeps on the veranda
by the sewing machines

- Senhor Santos, the tailors,
the clerk who does his letters,
his houseboys, the *ronda*,

and his brown daughters,
pretty in curlers, patiently
watching the road, awaiting

only an event.
Catfish, curled like tobacco,
are drying on a bench.

A limping mongrel licks
its yellow balls.
Sometimes the yard re-echoes

to a jeepful of soldiers
yelling out of their dust storm.
It settles on the hibiscus flowers.

Senhor Santos has long sideburns
and a straw hat:
his trouser leg is torn.

One glittering, domed night
he will wake to the drums
of freedom fighters.

He will go home
soon:
he will lose his yard of freedom:

he will mourn these vacant African afternoons.

Tales of the Islands
(after Derek Walcott)

1. Manchester Fête

If you see the fête! It had Jamaican,
Barbadian, Grenadian, Trinidadian,
Like they making they own federation in Englan',

an' one seta fellars from the li'l islands
like St Kitts an' them, where you cyan't run fast
or you go fall in the sea, an' all they just
calling theyself West Indian 'cause
what you ever hear 'bout St Eustacius?

But if you see the fête! O God, no rum!
no calypso! No steelban'! Is only
Guinness an' Rolling Stones! They play some
Sparrow tune 'bout English Society
an' take the record off 'cause it too crude.
Yes, man, is true! Those fellars too damn integrated.

2. Concert, Free Trade Hall.

Despers, we know that short for *Desperadoes
Steelban'*, it come *Gay Desperadoes* when those
Yankees study how you could sell they cokes
an' they frighten for a badjohn name, but look,
this *Trinidad Philharmonic Steel Orchestra* –
where you pick up that Afro-college culture,
Black Power classics by Johann Sebastian X?
What arseness you go be selling next?

Eh but those pans! That bass could really kick!
It have one double-tenor like the noteself talking.
Despers, is good you show these Englishmens
what you could do with they big famous tunes,
but I proud, proud you beat them j'ouvert style,
rough, fas', loud, like Laventille.

Briefs

1. In the Village

In the village
a deep debate.

The chief's daughter has a transistor;
she is dancing to the *Seekers*
gaily outside her hut.

But the tape-recorder man
on his codification project wants
"Your own music", he demands,
"Marimba! Bangwe!"

The chief is bemused
by this pressure from Europe
not to attend to Europe.

Is he 'himself'
with the radio on or off?

2. Moments Musicals

On a mudbank the reed huts
flood when the river is in flood.
We stop by the well and enquire. Bangwe?
A man is sent for. No good.
The instrument has gone for repair.

But money? He produces the bangwe,
a contraption of wood and wires

and bottle caps tied to a biscuit tin.
And look! He has changed his costume,
English rags to African tatters.

Squatting he chirrups and strums.
I smile. The fishermen twist with laughter.
He tells me he has finished. Blind
To his blindness, I toss a florin.
Too much, says my companion.

Noble savage: noblesse oblige.

3. Supermarket

Oh delicate are the white
arms and delicatessen shoulders
of the white wives leaning (oh
delectable their cool breasts)
forward, row of white wrists
arched in demand,
               and so
polite the black salesmen, such
un-negritudinal corncob smiles,
tendering
from pools of blood
delicious breast, liver, steak, chops, shoulders.

4. Indeed Of Course We Must All Respect

our customs,
said the businessman
leaning on the wing of his Mercedes,

our folklore,
said the lecturer
working another proverb into his novel,

our morals,
said the husband
burning the pamphlets and the mini-skirt,

our justice,
said the chief Chief
detaining his opponents without trial,

while the ninety-six per cent (all
indeed of course respect the four)
are elbowed to the edge of their own world.

5. When Livingstone Stared at the Lakeshore

When Livingstone stared at the lakeshore,
purging his boyhood in dreams of cotton,
did bouncing, honey-limbed girls
toss him a beachball?

When the presbyters broached their Galilee
with all hands psalming the Old Hundredth,
did they signal *The Moor's Head*
for whiskies and soda?

Visionaries, name-givers, lavish exiles,
reject their fantasies, but fear
that ulcered woman washing pots,
those blank, huge-bouldered mountains.

Dhow Crossing

*'Photographers should not miss Leopard Bay, where colourful
dhows land regularly'* (Malawi Holiday Guide).

The lake pitches in its void.
Invisible, the headlands
anchor a starless night.
A light winks from nowhere.
Watch. Faintly, the dawn glimmer
separates to a skyline.
The marked island bulges.

In morning, nondescript,
a washed-up coconut husk
bleaching on the horizon.
Watch. Slowly, as perfect shadows
shorten to the beach-huts,
it blanches, moon-struck.
But what? What-can-on-earth it's

birdshit! An island
ghastly with birdshit,
boulder and grass and brachystegia
shitlicked to a thin
icecap! Watch. Vaguely, heat
drains the bayscape
to sepia, but the island

glows like a presence, like
bones in flashlight
littering caves hyenas
have abandoned, or that eggshell
skull your fingers tip-touch
under the white shampoo
when your eyes avoid the mirror.

Memo: a colourful
subject for photography.
Watch. Ghostly, from such
absence, such a hole
in daylight (now sickening
to the yellow-green fluorescence
of fever trees), might not

dhows advance at dusk
rippleless on the chrome lake,
spectre slavers bonded
to enslaved ancestors?
All starless night the island
signals slave. I keep
expecting birdshit on my scalp.

For Captain Stedman

'I now must make an apology for my style, which is turn'd by G-d!
so very insipid, that I myself am tired with it. D-mn spelling. d-mn
writing, and d-mn everything overdone.'

1.

By G-d! Johnny, near pistoll'd
in your cradle, that pigeon's
crop you stuck up nanny's bum,
Jacobite schoolblows, raped
by your uncle's maid, and Mrs Mallet
tendering her carcass to an ensign,
lampoons and duels and haylofts,
punch and plackets, it makes
devilish fine reading!

and Joanna: not surprising
a mulatto slave girl be thrust
in somewhere, eh Johnny?
That's a ripe sketch you shape
of her, a ripe joke this nigger-
wench costlier than your fortune!
But wife? Two thousand florins?
A son? By G-d! Captain, that's
devilish unChristian!

2.

Therefore at L'Esperance,
the colony at war,
you built your house
of grass and wattle,
a room for your girl,
a room for painting,
a kitchen, henhouse,
palisades, a bridge.

Captain and artist,
wounded in the campaign,
you carved a pool
downstream under
the bamboo lances,
whose amber
drenched her body
sheerest gold.

Soldier and lover,
the revolt subdued,
you limped nightly

11

barefoot through
the mangrove's
gothic doorways
to the Dutchman's plantation
and her side.

A grass and wattle
studio at L'Esperance;
if only there were
diamonds, you prayed
searching upstream;
if only fighting
rebel blacks sufficed
to buy her freedom.

3.

Stedman, your Smollett-dabbed journal brags
loud of yourself, viz., I told the bugger
he ought to know a dog's turd from another
after getting so many, viz., I pass my time
making baskets for the girl I love, viz., d-mn
Order, d-mn Matter-of-fact, d-mn Everything!
and Captain you do, with five challenges
one month, no slight, no oversight, no lost
button or bruised bum too trivial to curse
and bring to cutlasses, yet such chivalrous
brawls, only with Captains! Johnny, you bore
a code in your fevers, far beyond Paramaribo
up brimming blackwater rivers where forests
choke in their creeper-hammocks, and Negroes
racked and handlopped, splintered on wheels,
hamstrung, scalded in sugar-vats, skewered

blistering by furnaces, and girls' breasts
mistress-whipped to blood for their masters'
fondling – Captain, your pen nib splutters Oh
Fie! for every gouge, brand, manacle, every
throat self-slit and earth eating, the horror
of nightly nightmares and Joanna's auction!

So what in the name of sketching are these
arabesques, these slender Egypt triangles
strutting the skylines of your history, viz.,
your *Narrative of a Five Year's Expedition*
Against the Revolted Negroes of Surinam?
Or these all-but nudes? such poised despair,
such healthy breasts and thighs! are they
slaves, these buxom Maori-haired Italians?
Or Joanna, your dear dead girl, whose wife-
maddening monument to five years' loving
on the Wild Coast your book is, how can
poison lie in ambush for this lilting virgin,
a straw hat in her hand, this barefoot
gipsy with the tight curls, her dark breast
proffered to a curving, friendly world
of formal palms and odorous orange groves?
Stedman, your gentle melancholy Art
Distills the loyal chaos of your heart,
Weeps o'er the victims of a barb'rous Age,
But distances to Elegance, Outrage;
You could not murder Style to match their Life;
You saw not Slaves but Men and a dear Wife.

13

Sinking

after level hours through
thick folds of darkness,
jolting on the tarmac,
the spirit flares streaming
yellow tongues towards the plane,
stepping into the cloth-warm
saltodorous night air
of a small swamp with a gate,
the cicadas shrill and clouds
buzz-buzzing every bulb
on the white-trunked avenue
of skeletal flamboyants,
hunched low in the musty
fan-shuddered terminal bar,

I am back where imagination
sank its first wells.

Gentler than Growth

Gentler than growth, Sahara
dust settles on the mango
leaves, and ruffian hotel
taxis, blaring in their
dustclouds, trail laterite
grit, drycoating eyes, daubing
brick-red this pot-holed
street of huts and lean-tos,
sulphurous pawpaws, rusting cane,
a red pepper settlement

of gardener, porter, sweeper,
waiter, bellboy and bargirl,
dancer and curio-man,
season ticket holders
on an endless middle passage.
As places go, this is a place
to turn back from, despite
coconut flags unfurling
bronze to rasp the corrugations
of the iron-bound chapel,
its summoning harmonium
querulous as mosquitoes as
my taxi barks rescue.

Briefly in the rear mirror
cloud and ash are radiant;
the travellers walk through fire
to their twilight Lord.

Correspondence

"Friend, we got here last November.
I'm writing (sorry to take so long)
slung across our veranda
in a hammock. You were wrong
about the climate. We're a thousand feet
above it, on a clifftop facing the sea.
The house (hardly a shanty) is fine
except for the ants and a stray cat.
It's pleasant as Alice serves coffee
to stare at the hulks in the estuary:
the castaway, his dusky concubine.

Man Friday too! in the squatting
shape of a schoolboy in the cupboard
downstairs. Rather fitting
really, since we can't afford
the tools it's meant for, so we store
him as lawnmower, spade and sickle.
He's used to it up-country
mixing his lessons with agriculture.
It's good as I down a six o'clock
beer to enquire about his kinsfolk:
the kindly proprietor, the peasantry.

Today, there's two! Musa's note
'Sounds or syllables can't carry
your kindness to my schoolmate'
was entertaining – and why worry
when new boy knows his stuff? He trapped
the watchman shitting in the drains.
He found out who at 3.00 a.m. coughed
filth under our bedroom – and it stopped!
It works at breakfast to confront
Pompey with yesterday's complaints:
The promising D.C., his handpicked staff.

P.S. April. Bribed to efficiency,
the police are quite certain. Musa,
says Pompey, has taken money.
We check, are short, he is dismissed.
This year we relax. After our deportation,
Pompey will laugh, sharing the beer
with soldier ants and the traitor
tomcat, staring in hammocked isolation
at shanties a thousand feet inferior,
and nobody will move up downstairs:
the one-party state, the cool dictator."

Province of Freedom

The Botanical Gardens (former
War Department Property Keep
Out, former bush) are

bush again, lianas wrapping
gun mounts and dog-Latin
tags, a python's grip

on ironwood and the cannon-
ball tree threatening the track
I carried Martin down

across the once-bridged brook
and up to Heddle's ruined Farm.
A viewpoint: easy to overlook

from here the plunging slum
of Freetown, or under this
shade tree where anthuriums

run wild now to erase
those shadow freemen, their
darkness like a bruise,

their dancing solitaire,
ankles shackled
to their record player.

Heddle's dreams of pastoral
composed this second garden.
Even now the sun angles

lightly through light-green
decks of guava, drenched
with bright flamboyant

down to this wooden bench
and Martin sleeping
in my arms. Branches

light with foliage keep
boughs heavy with flowers
raised, and I wrap

Martin tight, and stare
aloft through verdant arches;
it is peaceful here.

A viewpoint: but the watchers
(are there eyes behind
those shades?) approach:

they are not impassioned,
they are not impressed,
this is no-man's-land:

I fold my brown son closer to my breast.

Lusaka Blues

1.

After the salad afternoon
parties on the sloping lawn,
My Lady's hands and the Police
ensemble um-pah-pah in glove,
    After the dawn arrests, the sad
lucky deaths, and oh My Lady's
party for the Commissioners,
His Excellency's Last Post,
    After the limp flag has taken
Empire's last sundowner, and so
on etc., look out man, pull
off the road, here comes

the Party! In fifty-four
limousines: each car contains
one member, each member
has a driver, each driver hugs
an escort of five howling
sirencycles. Desolate the tarred road
to that settlement of Indian shops
the Party calls a city.

2.

Late afternoon we work in our separate gardens,
waving to each other from under lines of washing.
A lorry tours the estate collecting labourers.
The Party sirens are wailing on the airport road.
People will soon move into the redbrick flats

opposite the planned supermarket and petrol station.
There are swallows gathering on the telephone wires.
They look like heavy chords on a romantic score,
but whatever was once here has already departed.

Spain

It is May Day in Madrid, the old men march.
They are from Kent and Yorkshire. They shake
fists, chanting "Viva! Viva!" From among
the geraniums, the señoritas wave.

It is the old men's day. What world
did their ancient battles once occur in?
Hill Four-Eight-One, panting to the crest,
the enemies' faces white and visible.

Now they return, talking of thyme
and rosemary, and fallen comrades,
and of one absent, whose ashes
reverently they scatter under the olives.

Ordinary and old, today they swagger.
From red-splashed verandas, the dark girls
smile. Who does not admire them?
Which of us will passion keep so young?

Ministering

She has watched him rise and now he falls.
The radio denounces him. He returns
un-chauffeured, Benz-less, trudging the path
from the cotton depot where the lorry dropped him:
his paunch is heavy, his suit sweat-stained, he smells.

The children swagger in his wake. He mutters
at the anthills. It was tribalism, conspiracy,
his typists whoring. There was nothing else,
no reason. He was no different. The President
would learn things when he got his letter.

The path snakes through the village. What he didn't
see on the ministerial visit, in his soft world
of secretaries, his bitterness sees now.
The place is full of beggars, primitive, the thatch
rotting, reeds uncut, thistles in the cotton gardens.

She watched him rise. Now he returns. What accident
permitted it and what appetites propelled,
she knows. There is nothing to come back to.
The girls have gone, the young men have gone.
At the black door of her hut where burning cowdung

stuns the mosquitoes, she awaits her son.

After the Revolution

1.

Before the coup, this ice-cool water sprang
where the summit boulders punch the cloudbase, and it
fell, a smoking slipstream, swallowed
by ravines, issuing under the tree ferns
down slopes of brachystegia
to the cool shade-grevilleas and carpets
of lush tea, and this
pool poised on a ledge above
the shimmering dusty town. Before the coup
the occupying troops eased
guns from their shoulders, dangling
bare feet in the water. Today along the bush tracks
it is the liberators who are being ambushed.
From the deserted pool we watch
the cortege leave the barracks. The fusillade
echoes round the mountainside, dying
at the boulders where the ice-cold water springs.

2.

Hairy Dionysio, whose
missing eye-tooth isn't
mentioned by Euripedes,

malarial Dionysio, who
snared us with wine,
with pigeons for *petisco*,

kid-cutlets, giant
prawns, guinea-
fowl with coconut,

and brandy in
the lamp-lit store
he will not abandon

to the *Forças Populares*
throwing stones
at his paw-paws;

randy Dionysio, whose
brown, much-beaten
mistress bears

him annually
a child,
is perennial.

Across the road,
liberator Pentheus
is murdered;

there are new guerrillas
filing through
the tall grass.

Refugee

1.

Old warm boulders in the sunlight,
terracing the garden where the jacaranda
burns above a crumbling path of bricks.
She is young. There is a panic
of monkeys in the bamboo. Dry spears
tumble and are brushed off her hair.
She is young. After the violence,
the floorboards wet with bloodstains,
she blossoms here, climbing. The veranda
draws her upwards with its scented violets:
I greet her with a glass of coconut milk.

2.

The bombers strike, and shapes
in the photograph scatter, already dying:
the flames cling like water.
When the napalm
has eaten through their lives, only
bulldozers can assuage our horror:
the red trench swallows the charred corpses.

Bombers and grass huts,
and people in charity clothing queuing
for flour. It keeps raining
and is called revenge
for the tourists ambushed, the baby
hacked in bed, the burning
mission with its women raped and bludgeoned.

None of the guilty are killed:
the avaricious, the psychopathic,
the leaders, power-gluttonous.
But guilt, like human
flesh, clings. We eat, drink.
vote and read, and cannot honour
the graves or name a single murdered child.

3.

Secure in giving orders, when the gunmen
turned to face him he could not believe it:
these were his instruments, and he above
contention in his palace of corridors.
They too were nervous. His confidence
swelling to an order, they opened fire.

Drumming! The ebony, peacock crowds!
Largesse on the radio, the detainees
released. With luck, two season's
respite while authority remembers
the corpse in the corridor. Two whole rains
before IT grows secure in giving orders.

4.

Old colonial, burdened words
for this well-weathered house
and our pleasure in its charred

brickwork, its stone floors
glassy with age. Sunwashed
walls need no disguise

of creepers in the terraced
garden, whose mango and bamboo
and flame-cupped tulip trees

contain the broader view
of plain, lake and mountain,
quality in age the clue.

Colonial: we enlightened migrants,
visiting the battlefield,
knowing what demands

passed downhill from this old
house, dropping on the bare
heads of headmen and elders

for taxes and labour,
we mendicants, treading
the minefield, know

our legacy as nothing
so well built. Timelessly, bricks
burn. There is shooting

on the hillside. Our book
grows slowly to the steady
swift chiselling of the clock.

5.

Revisiting that house of terror
he found his anger burned away:
the blood-splashed floorboards were an error
which bloody dreams could not repay.

Now bombers shower the clustered tents
with napalm labelled retribution,
he honours all the innocents
for whom there can be no solution,

and boards his plane and flies in fear
to where the weaponry comes from:
the war will last another year,
but he is safe, and rich, and home.

Lark

At greylight, lark is up there
while night hugs the curbstones,
handful of bone and cartilage
blazing away like a transistor.

Has the fluttering creature crouched
hours in the lank verges,
lungs brimming with song?
At a glimmer, lark rises.

From the high dawn notes
shrill, precipitating
day. The motorway
hardens to light and noise.

Bar Domino

Bar Domino was the border;
the café tables addressed
another country halfway across the road.

Beyond the chickenwire and dust
of the backyard and the sideyard
were frontier posts,

rubber stamps and guards
and guns,
uniformly bored.

This left Bar Domino
nowhere
between the valley and the mountain,

and everywhere:
we came for what was banned
behind our barriers,

valley subjects for the tainted
air of Independence,
the hill descenders

for decadence,
and we, separately expatriate,
for freedom from our choices

in wine and heat
and talk and sex and prawns
while Macielle, like a deity,

dispensed.
All this, being years ago,
has its appropriate cadence:

the countries, grown bolder
in disagreeing to agree,
Bar Domino has been claimed and closed.

Some of us have a memory
of tubular chairs and beer mats,
the bottle-coloured mango tree,

leaves and dust
arguing in whirlwinds,
and after dusk

a sluggish fan
churning the fug, as metaphor
for all-man's-land,

vivid beyond the frontiers,
different from all we have
and are,

the violable origins of love.

From
The View from the Stockade
(1991)

Incident at a Poetry Reading
(for Eduardo White, *primo*)

In the old walled garden the young poets
have spread laden tables under the mango tree.
We stand reverently in the starving city

eyeing the roast suckling pig, samousas,
fried prawns, chicken with groundnut sauce,
goat piri-piri, wines and beers,

while the speech from the dais about the young
poets' aspirations reaches its peroration
in a *caldeirada* of revolutionary slogans,

and we clap, our hands straining to do
what they do next, reaching out for food
and drink until all the tables are cleared

and we stretch our legs under the mango tree,
a black silence in the glistening sky,
enjoying the young poets' newest poetry.

Eduardo is long-limbed. He bears signs
of his mother's tenderness. His sudden
manhood has tightened like a skin.

His poem is angry. The nation is a neglected
garden rank with rotting fruits. Corruption
and our silence are forfeiting victories.

We watch him touched on the shoulder
by uniformed men. He falters in his reading:
detention without trial has its own prosody.

But "talk!" they insist. "You are telling truths,"
and the poem ends wildly with kisses and applause
and the evening in an afterglow of pleasure,

beer bottles clinking in the mango tree's shadow,
talk about language and the international standard,
tiny green mangoes dropping on our bare heads,

while beyond the *bairros* past the airport road
despairing peasants flock to the city for food,
and the siege tightens with mutilation and murder.

Living in the Delta

       Darkness,
a wet tarpaulin weighing
down the mangrove, moulders
to a yellow fog, threadbare at dawn.
The fishermen stir from the fire,
their cigarettes trailing candleflies,
then slither narrow dugouts under
roots pale with oysters into the warm
crocodile waters of the creek.
After all these years of words it is still
discovery, the canopy whitening
over the surf, the silver glimmering beach,
and a medieval sea where pelicans
loom on a sandbank and these fishermen,
like the centuries, rock patiently
at anchor.

        Noon,
the sand vines blazing
purple and the white-hot sand
whistling to my heels, I found
her in the hollow where a coconut bole
strained at its roots, the palm's shadow
dark as the wreck's charred ribs
on the headland, clasping becalmed
the length of her olive body. She
to whom all metaphors return lay
strange and familiar, the gold
and tawny chevrons shifting only
to her breathing. Swamp, strand, the bayscape
taut as a drum.
        Dusk,
and a walk around the liberated
playground, the swing seats
unchained, the see-saw bending,
the toadstool tables turned. Feverish
in twilight, the estate house
crumbles. The Piper revs for take-off,
cantering down the golf course, barking
Scottie in pursuit. We along the flood
defences saunter to the club. Fires
glisten from the compounds where
shoeless children sing of blood,
their guns of bamboo slung across
bare navels.
        Night,
and the swamp road to *Hotel Chuabo*:
suits, fountains, canned music,
dinner like an airport café, varnish
flaking from the wardrobe door. But
Chuabo, meaning stockade, the town's

peasant name, has an eighth-storey
balcony for drinking. Far above
the masses, over the blacked-out *bairros*,
Russian experts, acrobats from Pyongyang
and we, separately expatriate, shuttered
with glass and the drifting stars,
meditate on the salt-logged coconut,
swamps of water hyacinth, the mouldering
steps at dusk where hippos boom
from the papyrus and the river lurks, waiting
its season, silted in the lifetimes
of some of us ... Each of us
rises in this stockade, far from ambush
and famine, to meet the kindly liberators.
They are correctly bearded and smiling.

Scribble

So the Swedes, the blonde gods, have abdicated,
the push-button saw-mill is abandoned.

In its twilight. mildew summons
vox humana of mosquitoes.

Outside in the day glare the far bank
fades to sepia, its fringe of palms dancing.

They were planning ho! ho! ho! these tall efficient
vikings with their bearded earnestness

that anthill and baobab, the river drifting with its
                             islands, the flapping herds

trumpeting down the mushroom huts and hut-high millet

be sawn, sanded, cooled, refined
to a white rectangle of paper like this one.

They are not the first
whose blank eden sprung a serpent.

Sugar men, copra men, tea, sisal, tobacco men
have all before loaded their ships and departed.

There are ruined engines of antiquarian value
corroding on all the river estates.

But nothing so fine as the saw-mill
shining blonde at the farm's edge, where a woman

hunchbacked with child is hoeing poverty,
still waiting for a god prepared to scribble.

From Robert Moffat's Journal, 1854

"4th June, Sabbath, the afternoon
cloudy and cold. Under the *mosetla* tree
I once addressed Senthuhe and his men.
The whole town has been burned off
by the Boers. No piles of stones,
broken pillars, tessellated pavements,
nor the shadow of a street, nor anything,
remain to tell 1000s once lived here.
Charred stumps peep here and there
through the ground, with two or three

skulls shot cruelly by the Boers,
and cats too, said one, watching my kittens.

Sebobi, hearing of wagons, came down
from the summit and his people emerged.
After coffee, I assembled them and preached.
I talked with him on the importance
of attending to divine things but, alas,
he is very far from the kingdom of God.

All will be ordered by Him who knows
our hairs' number and sees the sparrow fall
(there are no sparrows here. I had thought
them everywhere. Like flies and crows)."

Cotton, Rubber, Tobacco etc

"So now you are going to have your coffee?"
says the interpreter approvingly,
and the villagers gather in a noisy circle to study
the white man drinking his coffee.

They have all grown coffee for the white man
and can tell me about every stage
of the culture and preparation – except for the drinking
which is hilarious to watch.

Who knows? Next I might change my underpants,
blow up a condom, burn
a cigar, or do something else they have worked
lives for and never earn.

Chimwalira

The truth is he was born at Chimwalira
not Bethlehem. For Immanuel the conception
was a good one. But it was hard in a place
without writing to show prophecies fulfilled.
She gave birth on a reed mat in a mud house,
but so did every woman. How much grander
a stable signifying property in the foreground.
So when the Magi appalled by the Nile's
green wilderness turned back worshipping
a Jewish boy in a safe colony, they missed
their star's conjunction with Crux Australis
and God lay forgotten in Africa.

                                    Chimwalira,
"where someone died". He grew up ordinarily,
neither Tarzan nor Shaka, eating millet
and wild mice. After his circumcision
there were songs about his dullness with women.
He became a blacksmith and a doctor skilled
in exorcism, and people saw he was touched.
But there was nothing startling to the elders
in his proverbs. He died old at thirty-three,
a normal life span.

                     (It was the Reverend Duff McDuff
screamed the Python priest was the Black Christ
as they led him to his steamer in their straightjacket.)

Words for Heroes' Day, perhaps

Being in the Welsh style uninclined to give politicians
credit for the brilliant acts their speeches enjoin us
to applaud on their tightrope strung between banks,

nor finding congenial the climate of cenotaphs,
rituals of death as though death were sacrifice
and sacrifice legitimised those hierarchies of stamping,

not being, in short, in any sense *imbongi* or praise poet,
whether sweeping thorns from the ruler's path or brandishing
a symbolic knobkerrie as spokesman for the people,

I am in the English manner a little at a loss to find
words for this anniversary when visiting after Empire
I am asked to pay tribute to those who died for freedom.

That some were heroes is quite certain though not
necessarily the men on the platform (nor necessarily men).
Even the dead are ambiguous. Remembering them I think

most of those innocents cremated in their hundreds
as fire rained on the camps where they were queuing for flour.
Calling them heroes makes their slaughter seem called for

though their ghosts cry out for an eternal flame of anger.
Even among the warriors there were, as we too well understood,
the psychopathic who will never settle to justice.

But though irony has no heroes there is a poetry of facts.
There were others (not necessarily the men on the platform)
who are already legend and their legend a gracious one,

speaking of pastoral, the column filing through the tall
grass to a clearing with huts in the hut-high millet
and a shining welcome from the old who remembered the Rising,

speeches, courtesies observed with prayers to the ancestors,
songs and dancing, the girls crazy with admiration,
the meal from a shared pot when even a bean was divided,

then at moonrise moving onwards to the dawn's target,
and though doubting whether half of this happened or whether
half of that half matters in the unchanged city,

I honour them for the metaphors they died for. That
they made strutting ridiculous, if only momentarily,
is sufficient for our homage. May their ghosts

snatch at these anklets rattling today for our applause.

The Accord

The ambassador's wife greets with a kiss
Xavier, pot-bellied, hair growing out of his ears.

In his slim heyday he founded a dozen newspapers
and lost interest in them. The secret police

of six dictatorships had him on their files
though his insignificance kept him out of their jails.

Now he's a raconteur with a whisky in his hand,
a man to be courted, the right ear of the president.

He has been comrade to an alphabet of revolutionaries,
Amilcar, a true Marxist despite the controversies,

David who turned to the bottle when his poetry dried up,
Eduardo, Herbert, Marcelino, Philipe,

and Samora the victor whom, after fourteen years
of excoriating defectors, he advised to make peace

(though Nelson and Walter were still on Robben Island).
Xavier is writing a book about necessity and the dialectic

and his own career in cellars and public libraries,
those endless trains, third class, across central Europe,

and an article explaining about Dar es Salaam
based on Lazaro's letters and a diary kept at the time,

and a pamphlet analysing why the nation is in crisis.
The ambassador's wife is glassy-eyed listening to this.

The whisky bottle's hourglass has too long to run.
"How can you know," she says, "the right people will win?"

Xavier is disconcerted. He is not used to disagreement.
He was hardly aware there was a woman present.

"How do you stop it ending in a lot of nastiness?"
Is she a liberal? Or just stupid? A waste

of time explaining. He searches for Latin courtesy
just as she too is remembering necessity

and they smile like conspirators as she reaches
for the bottle, pours two fingers and signals the kitchen.

Theoretician-pragmatist, Xavier bows to the accord,
gets a peck at departure as his gallantry award.

Thief

The heat is on. We sleep
naked, starting at broken glass.

What will he feel the slippery
thief interrupted in the living room,

who has kept me hours by the smashed
door with this sharpened cutlass,

what will be his rage he grabbed
only the bassoon concerto K191?

Benighted under a toenail moon
the tin roof signs, contracting.

The fridge offs. In shocking quiet
a cockroach smacks the lampshade.

The nightjar whistles like someone
jumping sing-sing on a wire fence.

I am tuned for violence. I make
arpeggios with the cutlass. Images are

that head and hand through the jagged
frame and my striking bloodily.

Nightlong I appease witches.
With cockcrow the denials cease.

But what of him in his mud shack
in the *bairro* angry with Mozart?

Beauty, patronage, such order: shivering
he might well come back to kill.

From Episode in a War: Mozambique 1972

2.

Swamp and corrugation. She was not meant
to be outside. Five days they kept her
drugged in the customs house in the delta.
She lay on a white sheet in a cotton shift.
Five noons shimmered the island to sepia
squinnying her pupils though her blue eyes stared.
She was grounded metres above the river.
At dusk, husbanded impatiently, she watched
evening wrecked on a reef of coconut palms.
Day six, Ernesto shrank from his pale wife
getting drunk in a village near Mathilde
where satirical women opened their blouses
to give suck to the white man. That evening
she walked in her white shift to the beach.
Rust and detritus, the channel gouged
between hulks, the jetty a swamped freighter,
foredeck clutched by hands of mangrove, hold
bottomless with writhing embryos it had
dizzied her to stare down as she disembarked
while, sunk around her on the beach, sand
combed through her languid fingers was rust
of bolts, rivets, pipes, boilers, anchors,
buoys, steel plates, hinges, flaking, crumbling
like driftwood, dissolving. Clouds blazed
above the coconut flags. A dugout fought
the current with ringing solo and undertow
from six chanting paddlers. Flashes of pink
were flamingos returning. The first mosquito,
she stamped her name ISOBEL on the white sand
in the high tide slick where banana roots,
oil seeds, clumps of water hyacinth reeked
of reeds upriver where he forgot her baby.

4.

Ernesto woke with a headache on the mud floor.
He was going to beat that woman. He knew
what the terrorists did to Moises Ernesto.
They tossed him on their bayonets. They played
volleyball on the lawn with his little head.
He was a man. He had to exist knowing
such things. But she? A man needed comfort
when his baptised son was murdered, not
this deafening with silence. Go back
upriver? Fighting the current with the green
ambush waiting and the boy already dead?
His Excellency the Governor said, "Ernesto,
condolences, you did well to save the launch."
He was going to punish that woman. Not
tell her, that would be cruel. Only men
lived with knowledge. But teach her duty
like this woman with water from the river
and a rag to wash his prick and firewood
to roast his breakfast of mealie cobs – he
pulled her on top of him and rolled her over
and fucked her as she grumbled about children
and daylight. Well, she'd reason. He paid
extra. He enjoyed it more anyway, buying
these days.

     Walking home under coconuts
in the amber slatted light, he cursed
marrying her cotton chastity, remembering
the breasts of the mother of his sons.
They were all he had now. They weren't bad
kids, the little devils, and their mother's
breasts and her brown compliance – why
had he left them to marry this Portuguese?

Why, *por deus* had he spent his savings on
a wife from Vila Nova with her cold silence?
His boys were all he had now. He would
teach them volleyball, give them *his name*!
He walked on in wonder, his boot prints
crushing on the sand the marks of hundreds
of bare feet. Nothing had ever satisfied
like this revenge. A landrover honked
behind and he hitched a lift from a grinning
black corporal. "You kill any terrorists?"
"*Sim*, bwana. Three by the bridge this shining
morning. *Viva unidade! Viva the Republic*!"

The View from the Stockade

1.

From the stockade is a view of pastoral
lost, our fields and gardens
wasted by the enemy.

For years the city appalled us but
when the hordes came where
else was refuge?

From the stockade we watch thistles
swarm. We have our wives here
and water. We shall survive

all but the heartsickness, our innocence
undone. Now there begin
ledgerbooks, usury.

2.

"He's ca-ca-cantankerous," she stuttered.
It was her one English word
almost, and where in Yorkshire did she
find it, this Black woman
with her pig farmer, up
in the Dales? As she
woke at five, mucked out the sties,
she swore back in Acholi
with a ripeness his mind shut out.

"He's ca-ca-cantankerous," she stuttered
to the Race Relations men
in her distress. There was nothing
they could do but open a file.
Why had she followed him
home from the army? She had
nothing to go back to. What silks
did she expect? And he? What
had he hoped to harvest of his rutting?

3.

An old man striding, brittle in an anorak,
weathered as his walking stick, his wife
in a duffle coat, hand on his arm, together
halt in Sampson Square, once Thursday market.
"Once Thursday Market", he exclaims. "Aha!"
she says, brightening.
                              An old couple
discovering what they were looking for,
rhythms of pastoral in the traffic jams.

Joanna

1.

The hardest part, writing the account
A dozen years after in a another country,
The hardest memory was her utter
Separateness. She had lain in his arms
So soft, so pliable, he was the bridge
Straining above her, drowning
In her depths as she ebbed to the sea.
He was the leaky dam at L'Esperance.

Writing the account, her death made
Believable his lost age of gold.
But he knew it was never so. For
All the rich tapestry of poems
He wove round her, a fuck
Was a fuck. It left her untouched.

2.

I was slave, not so? The hardest
Part was he touched me with hope.
Not in bed as he pounded me
With his soft pestle, but after
When sweettalk could get him no more
And he sang his poems. He built me
A pool at L'Esperance by the gold
Waterfall. I loved him, nearly.

But he's just a man. No money, like
My father. Soon he'd want younger
Girls to pound out his pride, and where
Would I hide in England? So I laughed.
When he married I smashed my mortar
And drank my poison. And felt sure.

On the Train, Reading Dante.

Halfway along the line we have to travel
I found myself in a siding outside Doncaster:
the sky was darkening, the land was level.

Both sides were fields of industrial waste,
black water, derelict caravans.
To halt there and know the place exhausted

brought on the old despondence.
Nothing so fine as wolf, lion or leopard
(that's money, pride or concupiscence,

piquant temptations!) stood
in the track. Nor was I in control
the diesel waiting at red.

As when the slaver's musket barrel
flashed in the torchlight and the cave
grinned with its cache of skulls,

the faces of corruption came alive.
Nearest the mouth, Appetite
with a toadstool as hors-d'oeuvre,

wheeling its basket from the hypermarket
while the swollen-bellied, knob-
jointed world's children cry out.

Second skull, Theory, a spider's web
spun taut across the eye-holes:
mechanical and merciless its drab

dialectic. Next resident, Malice,
smirking from a ledge (what minister fixed
him there?) at blades and fibulas

scattered on the cave floor, a chalk wrist
reaching out, encircled by its amulets,
supplicating Treachery, Violence

and Fraud. I remember the clay pots
of millet beer, left in the entrance hole
to propitiate such malignant ghosts

as Dante Alighieri wrote to kill.
How thoroughly, without melodrama,
he marked down the lineaments of hell.

How solidly they live doing harm
to people who are known to me and I love.
Staring at my darkness I was calmer.

Then somewhere something happened, and I was moved.

On a Painting by William Etty

Towards the end he painted
pheasants, plumed iridescent
cock and drab hen together
limp with apples and mirrored nuts
on an oak table.
                              This was
long after London, his vast
canvasses of allegory, when

Truth and Chastity came to Fall
with breasts so veined, so rosebud-tipped
impropriEtty they joked.
                              The journeyman
homed to Yorkshire where the gentry
gunned pheasants. There is all
sadness in this shattered
wing, fuschias, purples, yellow
accusing iris.
                              Towards
the end he painted miniatures,
girls' faces mapped
with autumn, and these
stiffening overdressed game birds,
fruits, fruits.

For her Wedding She Wore her Breasts Bare

For her wedding she wore her breasts
bare with woven beadwork at her waist
and plaited beadwork in her hair.
The girls sang, begging her
never to leave them for the bridegroom's mat.
Her heart soared as they drew her to his hut.

In Leeds she wears a duffel coat and headscarf.
Her straightened hair is shielded from the rain.
Her husband at the Poly studies husbandry.
He is proud his village wife wears dungarees.
She pushes her packed trolley round Tesco's,
black, pregnant, angry, missing

cowdung smouldering in the soft dusk as
cattle praises echo from the kralls.
The woodsmoke curls from cooking fires.
The children demand stories
or a lick of the ladle. Darkness drops.
The men come home in blankets with their pipes.

From The Highjack: an Epithalamium.

2.

Full moon, guard her as she flies:
the air hungers
at such height: the cylinder
holding her is fragile:
no one knows what winds lurk
to whirl her into what spirals.

Full moon, as she flies, protect
from summoning desert,
swamp and jungle: ice
furs and clamps movement:
who can tell what armies wait
exacting what revenge for insult?

Full moon, shield her as she flies,
shine with superior
innocence on accident
and fevered malice: soot
seduces from the rooftops:
Goddess, light her swiftly home.

6.

Beyond them all
was the forest
humming with spirits:
in a sunlit clearing
houses with reed
walls and plaited roofs,
and the farms
spreading like green lakes.

Beyond them all
was the river
with green islands
turning in the current:
on the river
paths at dusk
women slender
with waterpots.

Cockcrow and children
and the husbands
planting, and wives
again to the river
as smoke unwound
from cooking fires.
In the forest
humming with spirits

crouched the hunter
with his charms:
duiker smooth
as an old hoe,
chimpanzee the drummer,

and buffalo before whom
unrequited the hunter
prostrates himself.

When they came
upriver by steamer
home, he was
ambushed by memory.
Within us all
is the forest,
the sunlit clearing
with houses and woodsmoke,

self-sufficient,
the generations talking,
the circle unbroken
by travel or trade.
Innocence dies
hard in the lover
when forests advance
on the spiked palisade.

Briefs

1.

I put my pen down for a lunch of goat's cheese,
bread, last year's wine and a melon, looking out
across red-tiled terraces to fishing boats
back this morning hours before I bought bread watching
the groomed and ironed girls trooping lovely to the city
and came home to writing. Then a siesta,
a walk and writing. I am doing
what I should like to do for ever. No,

there will be no second stanza questioning
this. These and children and you blossoming
like morning glory on walls everywhere
are all a man could need, and paper. As for
the makers of bread and red wine, I would
trust them for life beyond the purveyors
of varnished cork tiles or fish tanks or plastic
flowers in the hypermarket on the Marginale.

2.

"The most difficult art in the world," said
the *administrador* between mouthfuls, squid-prodding

fork raised, his right hand casting for the English words
(I thought of *ottava rima* and Camões)

"is the art of choosing a good melon."
Camões sits in his square under the pigeons:

his poetry is fired hard like tiles:
his round eye ridicules the end of empire.

To be fair to my friend (retired) the grilled squid
was succulent in the club where they planned the coup.

Everything that summer was like the wild melons
exploding at a touch to scatter seeds.

3.

I parked outside the hospital in *Luis de Camões*
and waited. I was coaxing alive a poem.

Two men with a coffin went inside:
fifteen minutes later I had changed a tense.

Four men, two in tee-shirts, one with a cigarette,
shouldered the coffin into the hearse. The two stood back,

dusting nothing from their hands, easing their shoulders,
refusing thanks "for nothing", and crossed

the road to the café, ordering *aguadente*.
The poem clicked suddenly like a shut box.

4.

Late summer brought Atlantic gales:
the beaches whitened, charcoal fires

flew wild. Behind our shutters we talked
suddenly of winter. Research

reveals, announced the team on TV,
there are 2229 basic Portuguese words.

Artur and his children came to dinner:
jailed by one side, exiled by the other,

he has been angered into cold action.
Afterwards at the window I ate grapes

spitting seeds into the swirling darkness.
Across the square under the flapping awning

a man and woman lingered over wine.

Surfaces

(for Jill & Alberto Dias)

I like the cool tenor of tiles:

the coolest place in *Largo de Camões*
is the tile shop. More even than the *livrarias*,
dusty and cavernous with riches, it holds us.

There is the sea in tiles:

dolphins, wine-carriers, marketers, lilies,
discoverers and farmers,
are transfixed and transfigured

in a poetry of blue squares.

While the jangling trams snarl and gross fish
leer from the restaurant windows,
the houses are quiescent.

Tiles have burned their passions out:

they bring us back to surfaces, to dark wine,
a green bottle on a table cool with glaze,
afternoons of light and patterns:

tiles can be wiped clean endlessly.

Do Tempo Perdido
(after Sebastião da Gama)

Before we left I watched for two hours
darkness closing on our golden beach.
It began with the cliff's shadow

sliding along the bright sickle, touching
the bathers and the lovers who rose
separately and dressed. It stretched

out across the emerald waters so
clear you could stare
down fifty metres and see

the fishing boats silhouetted
on pale sand. You could see mackerel
hovering and the drifting tresses

of water plants. Then darkness clicked
and the sea became only the mirror
of an olive sky and of lights flickering.

I watched for an hour the colours
of that surface. Perfection
and effort and error

are a loss beyond irony.
I could see houses and the fishing boats,
whitewashed and pantiled, or painted

every colour, giving out lights
all present in the poem
of the sea's surface, and defeated.

Olive became pewter, hardening
to blacklead, and still
the oil murmured.

I asked for the bill
and you wrote a cheque
and we struck the steep hill

into the night without speaking.
From the summit
the sea was a void, beckoning.

Lamps in old vineyards
blessed our hurtling
down converging valleys to our bed.

Antonio Rui

Antonio Rui whose township mother was always,
grinned the white managers, available
                              if you were desperate,

Rui, born in the *bairro*, father unknown,
with a cleft palate, a game leg, and sores
                              corrupting his eardrums,

would hobble the track between tin-roofed shanties
where women sweated at mortars, or dragged behind them
                              huge water barrels,

with a watch strapped to his left wrist, a transistor

clapped to his right ear, gold teeth smiling, his shades
                                        reflecting coconut palms,

and jabbering, stammering in tortured Portuguese
of a Grundig next year, a Suzuki, an outboard motor,
                                        a Boeing 747 to Lisbon,

and we shared the joke. What worked and gleamed
he worshipped. People being flawed irreparably, polished
                                        gadgets were his icons.

Today, years on, earphones, Grundig, digital watch,
we met him hobbling in *Largo de Camões*, as voluble
                                        with images as ever:

next year he will cross the Tagus, next year
a beach house for his mother, next year the white men
                                        will make him *chefe*.

Charcoal

There is a moment when the wood has caught
and the charcoal has done its tinkling
and glows lasciviously, when
the carafe of *Dão* or *Quinta da Bacalhoa*
simmers in our talk
of long delayed summers peering
down at long last down
our well between the terraced houses
north north north
on our tiles and towel of lawn,

there is a moment when the fumes of burning
lamb with oreganum, bay leaves and onions,
drift across the rag of lawn
to the brick wall where I'm reading
Walcott or Sebastião da Gama
or Dafydd ap Gwilym slagging
January, purring over May
and his burning trysts
in the improbable holly bush,
at that moment all our summers merge

in a scent so quick I don't know
what I'm remembering but, before
reductive words, happiness
floods, stinging my eyelids,
and I walk to where you are turning
skewers and I hold
your waist while you press
my wrists with your elbows:
all summers with wine and charcoal
are dark with south and south is you.

Immortal Diamond
(Jack Mapanje, detained 25 September 1987)

Outside the bar, night, bullfrogs promising rain,
the sky a dome of stars ripped
by the black edge of the mountain.

Bloated face, trunk like a baobab,
"We've got your lame friend,"
from the unmarked jeep

boasting special branch. Words hidden
a hemisphere off grudge
"Now you're on your own,"

and I can smell here the Carlsberg
on his breath. He leers
from the smuggled page.

Lame: alone: "we're
preparing a place for him."
This clown knows the power

of pauses, the ecstasy of rhythm.
His threat is accurately
their dread. For Jack, our dear friend's poems

are out, unparoled, his meta-
phors dancing from lip
to lip and no heavyweight

knuckles ripping
pages
can stop

them. The crippled swagger
"We've got your friend,"
calms outrage

at that night, that frog-loud prison yard, leaned
on by the mountain, where Jack, joke, patch,
matchwood, hardens

like starlight, needing no crutch.

From
Bounty
(1993)

Prescript: Landfall

HMS Dolphin: 1767

June 20: At 9 A.M. we was oblidged to laye to,
espetially as we heard the sea Bracking and making
a great notice on some reefs of Rocks. In a short time
the fogg cleared up, and we now suposed we saw
the long wishd for Southern Continent so often
talkd of, but neaver before seen by any Europeans.
The country had the most beautiful appearance its
posable to Imagin, with great numbers of trees with
flowers of various colours which must certainly bear
some sort of fruit yet unknown to us – but I shall drope
this Discourse as no good spy Glass discovered it to me.

We saw upwards of a hundred canoes betwixt
us and the brakers all padling off towards the ship.
When they came within pistol shot they lookt at our ship
with great astonishment, and padled round and made
signs of friendship to us, holding up Branches of Plantain,
and uttering a long speech of near fifteen minutes.
Some of the sailors Grunted and Cryd lyke a Hogg
then pointed to the shore – oythers crowd Lyke cocks
to make them understand we wanted fowls.
This the natives of the country understood and Grunted
and Crowd the same as our people, and pointed to the shore
and they brought a good many fine young Girls down
of different colours, some was a light coper colour oyrs
a mulatto and some almost if not altogeather White –
This new sight Atract our mens fance a good dale,
and the natives observed it, and made the Young Girls
play a great many droll wanting tricks, and the men
made signs of friendship to entice our people ashoar.

All the sailors swore they neaver saw handsomer made
women in their lives, and declard they would all to a man,
live on two thirds allowance, rather nor lose so fine
an opportunity of getting a girl apiece – even the sick
which hade been on the Doctors list now declard
a Young Girl would make an Excelent nurse and they
were Certain of recovering faster under a Young Girl's
care nor all the Doctor would do for them.

All this time the Bay was lined round with men, women and children,
to see the Onset which was near at hand. But they
still behaved freindly until a large double canoe
came off from the shore. with several of the Principle
Inhabitance in her. This canoe was observed to hoist some
signal and the very instant all trade broke up, and in a few
secants of time our Decks was full of Great and small
stones, and several of our men cut and Bruisd. This
was so sudden and unexpected that we was some time
before we could find out the caus. We then found
Lenity would not do, therefor applyed to the Great Guns
and gave them a few round and Grape shot which struck
such terrors amongs the poor unhapy wretches that
it would require the pen of Milton's self to describe.

After all this orders was given that the Boats set out,
and in a few minutes Landed and formd on the Beach,
and with hoisting a Pennant took possession of the Island
In His Maj name, and Honourd it with the name
of our Most Gracious sovereign King George the third.

1. The Hearing

The case is Christian's mutiny. But your court
won't stomach that *Christian*. It smells of
mercy. This tale's awash like the *Bounty's*
bilge with meanings no one wants. We were all there, you
all saw, Adams, black Matthew, gunner Mills,
by Christ, Adam's mutiny! Jack Adams, John Doe,
every-man-Jack's mutiny! But your Lords
need a hanging, not this tale rippling
Irishly like a stone in a green lagoon.

I remember the white untidy beach, my head
a washed-up coconut jumping with sandflies.
If my fiddle were jailed and not fathom
five in the Barrier reef singing to catfish
I'd strike up a jig the court martial
would dance to! Michael Byrne, Irish fiddler,
two thirds blind, on trial for my life.

> *I kissed that maid and went away.*
> *Says she, young man, why don't ye stay?*

George Stewart, midshipman. That's a truly
life matter. Gentle George, drowned in leg-irons
in a panic of keys while your Captain Edwards
jumps ship as light and easy as he's danced
from your court. Tacks his ship on the coral?
Huzzah! Drowns his shipmates? Well away!
And George's bounty, sweet brown Peggy, who
ever chose a better wife in the South Seas
or England? Crouched on the poop by the cage
keening and I could smell the blood, George
heaving at his chains yelling she was bloodying

67

the baby and us cursing double Edwards
she was after carving open her scalp
with a shark's tooth.

All dark his hair, all dim his eye,
I knew that he had said goodbye.
I'll cut my breasts until they bleed.
His form had gone in the green weed.

Did she see her midshipman dead in Edward's box
on Great Barrier Reef?
A life matter truly! And now I recall
the oath he swore her in Matavai Bay
he'd never again set foot in muddy
England with its watery sun and broomsticks.
That sweet sundown with the wind offshore
drunk with blossoms no white man had named,
he held up his left arm to my better eye
and I squinted at a heart with a dart
through it and a black star. "What's this?"
I warbled, and he says "tattoo." Took him
all day and hurt like blazes. But permanent.
One of their words, tattoo. Strange how we
needed their lingo to make a landfall.

English boy, please tell to me
What is the custom in your country?

The new Cythera. Two volcanic breasts
and a fern-lined valley. Half a league
leeward you'd miss it. I'll say this for Bligh,
in the whole South Seas he'd smell out one
breadfruit tree on a rock. But Tahiti
scuttled us. There were oceans we couldn't

sail and that island named them: taboo.
Another locution we harboured. We're all
marked with Tahiti, hearts and stars
and commemorations. You, Millward, is it
God's truth you've Tahiti's chart on your yard
and compasses? Morrison, scratching your
journal of excuses, is your loving groin
gartered with *Honi soit qui mal y pense*?
How d'you hope to escape hanging after
pledges like that? Leave Bligh out of it,
truly the only blind man in Tahiti,
a pool fool with his rules and longitudes
while Michael Byrne, fiddler, kept watch.
Taboo: Christian's mutiny. Ten of us
Of twenty-five still waiting to be hung.

> *King Louis had a prison,*
> *He called it his Bastille,*
> *One day the people tore it down*
> *And made King Louis kneel.*

2.   **The First Man**

Tahitohito,

        the Fifth Age when
        cunning gave birth to mockery.
               First
Was Ta'oroa the egg, tired of loneliness,
and his wife Stratum Rock,
Ta'oroa of sure bidding, of the cloudless sky,
        who stood over the passage of the reefs.
Ta'oroa was a god's house, his backbone
        the ridgepole, his ribs the buttresses.

Ta'oroa married his daughter Moon
                and moulted red feathers from which grew
                all plants except breadfruit tree.
Ta'oroa conjured Shark God and Rooster
                and Octopus who clasped
                earth to sky, smothering all light until
Ti'i stood forth, the first man,
                and was angry,
Ti'i the boat-builder, clothed in sand,
                was angry demanding
Light and he wrestled with Octopus' eight forearms
                till sky floated free
                shining with starlight and sunlight.
Then Ti'i the fire-maker, the axe-sharpener, was hungry
                and his oven was sealed at daybreak
                and opened at nightfall
                but the meat was raw because
Sun was made drunk by space and hurtled like a meteor
                until Maui his firstborn
Roped his ten rays with ten anchor cables
                and day became a task's length
                and order was complete.

4.   The Kindest of Fathers

The Second Age was of trouble when nobles settled
                the high headlands
                and the gentry the quiet bays
And the commoners encroached everywhere, breaking
                down the bamboo fences of the great.
Then there came famine, so cloudless even the chiefs
                ate land crabs and red clay,

But Ruata'ata, kindest of fathers, led his wife and children
                    to the mountains to gather ferns
And taking pity, his toes rooted and his fingers branched
                    and he became Breadfruit tree
Heavy with ripeness and his family feasted, and so trouble
                    gave birth to wisdom.

7. South

The Pacific, wept by God in his blindness.
You'd steer twelve months on a half-wrong tack
and never hear breakers, the sun dangling so
high above the main mast even I squinted.
In the end the look-out was singing Ahoy
when birds appears, petrels and albatrosses.
They'd a trick of calling up a south wind
and at cockcrow we were among islands.

> *On the Bounty were the rules*
> *Pump ship, packet ship,*
> *Not for soft and silly fools*
> *In the South Pacific.*

This wasn't discovery. Cook knew 'em already
and that Frenchie they call Buggerville. From
Deptford Dock to the Spithead cathouses
we'd all whistled for the brown girls so
wet for sailors they'd do it on the beach
with their uncles watching. What we disputed,
Tom Birkett and me eight bells to four
by the lagoon where we supped on green mussels
and Muspratt swore the devil he was poisoned,
was AD 1773 carved on a trunk. A footprint

like Defoe's island. Where was that and whose
knifework was it? Our first landfall we were
tracking ourselves, imagining shipwreck.

> *Never was there heard a word*
> *Pump ship, packet ship,*
> *Of the crew that stayed on board*
> *In the South Pacific.*

9. Breadfruit

Nippled in your palm and heavy,
sweating like a green swamp.

> *I put my hand upon her thigh,*
> *Says she, Young man, ye're rather high.*

10. Tahitohito

So *Bounty* dropped anchor and we swaggered ashore
        girls draped on our necks
In the Fifth Age, *tahitohito*, when cunning
        gave birth to mockery.
They twigged at once we were the right gods
        for the times.
Our tricks with a foresail made 'em stare
        and our iron was like gold.
But nothing we did showed reverences, and we
        fucked anything that moved.
Then the ballads started. Cook's men were back,
        bleached like lepers,
Stinking like stale milk, our hides tattooed

with brawling and the cat.
It confirmed the revolution and what better cockshy
than Bligh himself
With his martinet's livery and his wooden wife
in *Bounty's* figurehead?
We were *tahitohito*, the Fifth Age, and their worship
was disbelief.

12. Bligh

But how would old Bligh consider himself
politic? Show him seven skies of stars, he'll
prick 'em. But when he stalked the beaches
in full rig, sweating rank through his spine
and armpits, you'd hear *wei-wei, tahitohito*,
and hoots of belly laughter.

> *Who's the thief?*
> *Tareu the thief*
> *Stole Bligh's anchor-buoy.*

Their women
got nowhere, not even Queen Purea who knew
she was better bred and made it statecraft
to service her. But this was another
Cook, besotted with his ship. Fingering
Bounty's timbers was stroking his woman.

> *I put my hand upon her hip,*
> *Says she, Young man let's take a trip.*

What crazed 'em were the iron goods and muskets
he showered on mad chief Pomare – so much
it took a mansize sea chest to shut 'em in

with a padlock and clasp, Pomare's people
not troubling overmuch about ownership.
But Bligh's temper did the rest. When they saw
what tantrums they could wind him to over
tin pots or a thimble they'd him snared.
Before the end they were pocketing his crew.
They took George Stewart and Churchill, Millward
and Muspratt. They'd ways of thieving the heart
from your breastbone Bligh could never police.

October's moon they made their play. The *Arioi*
were in town, warrior actors with crimson
thighs and feather skirts driving the women
crazy with admiration. The *Arioi* could say
what they liked and take what they liked and we all
buzzed how they'd lampoon Bligh. It started
on the *Bounty* with Bligh feeding Pomare
like a nanny through seven courses of pork.
Upside down, you see, everything reversed.
Then we rowed 'em ashore and hoisted 'em
under the coconut arches to a clearing
with so many bonfires the *Arioi* called it
sun-copulating-with-moon. Aye, I was
there, with my bum at a fireside and a fistful
of ribs my fiddle had earned me, marvelling
how on that island I could always make out
candleflies, like scatters from the sunsets
that had me blinkered. But Bligh was an extra.
They kept him waiting, watching their play.
There were actors who weren't actors, *Arioi*
who weren't *Arioi* acting, and their argument
was theft. They sat feasting, keeping Bligh
in audience, till one of 'em would sneak his
neighbour's pork-knuckle, and they bounced up
and danced in a line:

Who's a thief?
Tarue the thief
Stole Bligh's rudder.

So they turned Bligh
overseer, and perched at their feast again,
till someone colonised a breadfruit slice:

Who's a thief?
Tarue the thief
Stole Bligh's compass.

Then they changed their burlesque, from Bligh
without bearings to Bligh the woman-hater.
By Christ, I loved it. They're blinder to books
than Michael Byrne but they read their enemy.
Bligh shouldered the baskets and bolts of calico
and the suckling pig he'd been told to bring 'em
back and forth from the cutter like poor Jack Tar
to the Big Men staring down from the platform.
There were nine of 'em, lounging on their stools,
twirling their toes and languid fly-whisks, frowning
like judges at a fart till one of 'em sang out:

I am the comedian of this land
That vibrates with the gun.

He uncurled, all seven foot of him, strutting
like a bird of paradise and taunted Bligh,
husband of the *Bounty*, hater of thieves,
whether he'd children in his own country. So
there was Bligh, untouched by woman, confessing
to fatherhood and, by God, they made him lumber

back to the cutter for a second forfeit.
This time they'd a speech for him. Pomare
cued him line by line and he thought 'twas his
accent convulsed while the *Arioi* sat deadpan:

> *This is the age without meaning,*
> *No payment, just copulation,*
> *Copulation to climax, one after another.*
> *The mouth does not even have to call out,*
> *The eyes say all that is necessary*
> *Until we have made our circle of Tahiti*
> *Copulating, copulating, copulating.*

Bligh stood there cunning in his livery
with the crowd whoop-whooping at every line,
but he couldn't see ourselves in their mirror.
The man thought he was diplomatising, getting
Bounty pregnant with breadfruit on the cheap.

17. Oro

Even the gods hadn't foreseen this Sixth Age
                          of Horrors
When breadfruit tree's shadow, shook by Ta'oroa,
                          moved across Hina-the-Earthbound
And she grinned up at the shade which instructed her
                          "Here are Ta'aroa's genitals,
Stand and examine them and insert them."
                          So Oro was born.
                          Oro the rabid pig
One jaw pointing to the sky, the other
                          to the red earth, gaping
For "man-long-bananas" on his altar of skulls,

Oro the sixth finger,
Bandaged bloodily, on the left hand
                of Tahiti the fish.

18. The Action

After your mutiny 'twas a different island.
It made fresh fools of all of us except
George and sweet Peggy. I danced to Papara,
crazy about the *Arioi* and women, keeping
downwind of your battles. Old Purea
liked my fiddle, and I'd as sound a perch
on a canoe in her courtyard as on *Bounty's*
capstan. I never knew they'd coined Oro
in our mould. When you'd your way, Morrison,
and made that dunce Pomare king, the eyes
gouged from the sacrifices plucked even
mine open. Christian's *noblesse oblige*
made 'em noble savages. Now they were
primitives and we'd guns.

> *Mit mein niggerum, buggerum, stinkim,*
> *Mit mein niggerum, buggerum, stinkim,*
> *Vell, ve'll climb upon der steeples*
> *And ve'll shit down on der peoples.*

You want me to sing of your wars, Morrison? I can track you
in my twilight, scratching at your book
of righteousness. I know what you're thinking
to flatter your Lords with. The poor natives
needed government, did they? You'd found out
they were tribesmen and tribes are hooligans
in the wise reign of our George. That island

glowed with its bellbirds and candleflies and the sea
in the casuarinas and the courtyards you'd
dawdle into and squat on a stump and with
two bars of "Willow, willow" have everyone
quiet as breathing. For you, 'twas for sieges,
stratagems, night marches and ambuscades,
your stinking groin gartered with *Honi soit*,
and for what blunt end? To make Pomare
king with his wits as addled as our George's!
That's princely flattery, Morrison. That'll
buy you reprieve.

> *Tweedle-Dee*
> *And Tweedle-Dum*
> *Bow your head*
> *And raise your bum.*

So Tahiti's tribes came
against you like they'd never hated Bligh,
pitching down the mountainsides from the nor-west
and west and all points of the compass south
in a real mutiny, one that knew its business.
Only your guns succoured you while Pomare
clapped his ears against the bang bang of murder.

Don't boast you'd no hand in it. I heard you
at Parara when Pomare despatched
his coronation standard and people smothered
their cooking fires and hid in the forest. You
saw for all its feathers, 'twas the Union jack
and barked fusillades in King George's honour.
English colours, English powder.

Pop-pop went the muskets,
Bang went the gun,
Crash went the cannon
And out went the sun.

                    Those last days
on Tahiti, we all traipsed like schoolboys
to the temple Pomare had built for Oro,
the war god your taboos bestowed on him.
All your tribes submitted. Only Vehiatua's
people raised their skirts and bared their arses
at your flag. The rest looked to the mountains
when their children were speared through the right
ear and dragged behind canoes to Pare
and flung before the new king of Tahiti
who sat with his mouth open while the priests
skewered their eyeballs with bamboo splints.
                    Aye, it's true,
Pandora saved you, Morrison. Double Edwards,
of all captains, arrested you in your frenzy.

Postscript: Landfall

HMS Beagle: 1835

October 20: At first light, Tahiti
was in view. As soon as we anchored
in Matavai Bay, we were ringed by canoes.
This was our Sunday, but the Monday
of Tahiti: if the case had been reversed,
we should not have received a single
visit, for the injunction not to launch
a Sabbath canoe is strictly obeyed.

She wears red feathers
And a hoola hoola skirt,
She wears read feathers
And a hoola hoola skirt.
She lives on
Just coconuts
And fish from the sea,
A rose in her hair
A gleam in her eye
And a love in her heart for me.

Everyone brought conch shells for sale.
Tahitians now understand money and much
prefer it to parrot feathers or nails.
The various coins, however, of English
and Spanish denomination puzzle them;
they never seem to think the small silver
quite secure until changed into dollars.

I work in a London bank
Respectable position,
From nine to three
They serve you tea
But ruin your disposition.
Each night at the music hall
Travelogues I'd see
And once a pearl
Of a native girl
Came smiling right at me.

There are many who scorn the missionaries'
improvements and dub Presbyterian the ban
on night revelry and the nose flute.
Such reasoners never compare the present
island with that of twenty years ago. They
forget, or will not remember, that human
sacrifices, an idolatrous priesthood,
profligacy unparalleled, bloody wars – all
these have been abolished: and dishonesty,
intemperance and licentiousness reduced.

Tired of the London bank
I started out a sailing.
Fourteenth day
From Mandalay
I spied her from the railing.
She knew I was on the way
Waiting, and was true.
She said, you son
Of an Englishman,
I dreamed last night of you.

Queen Pomare was persuaded to dine
on the Beagle. Four boats were sent
and the yards manned on her Majesty's
coming on board. The Tahitians behaved
most properly. They begged for nothing
and seemed content with their presents.
The queen is a large, graceless woman
with only one Royal attribute: a perfect
immovability of expression under all
circumstances, and that a rather sullen one.
Rockets were fired. After each explosion
a deep "ah" echoed from all points
of the moonlit bay. Our sailors' shanties were
much admired. Of one, the Queen declared
"It most certainly could not be a hymn".

I'm back here in London town
And though it may seem silly,
She's with me
And you should see
Us stroll down Piccadilly.
The boys at the London bank
I know they hold their breath.
She sits with me
And drinks her tea
Which tickles them to death.

Unwittingly, I was the means of my companions
breaking their own laws. I had with me
a flask of spirits, which they could not
refuse to partake of: but as often as they
drank they put their fingers before their
mouths, and uttered the world "Missionary".

**From
South
(1999)**

Poetry of Verandas

(for Helen and Hélio Álves)

1.

Here's evening, pinesmoke
with shafts of gold,
the sheer well-being
of a mosquito bite.

On the third floor we are
up among birds, not
the caged canaries but
martins veering so
tight I could grab them
like Jehengir Khan who caught
the swallow at Lords.

In the haze, a pigeon
stutters by, anxious
and out of his depth.

Come, poetry,
smoulder, lascivious
as charcoal, target
the ear like senhor mosquito,

zoom like the martin's
shadow, skimming
tessellated pavements, leaping
houses, somer-
saulting, can
turn on an *escudo,*
is most feigning
in its scything graphite
when closest to matching
the uncatchable.

2.

For Luís Vaz de Camões, then, how was it
quarantined just down there off Cascais
all-but-home after seventeen Christmases
the plague raging, Lisbon a necropolis,

how did he feel the colonial voyager
with his vision of Portugal, his *octavo*
epic sundried and nurtured through
mutilation, fevers and shipwreck

in the bag? Was the court corrupter
than he recalled, the clergy more ignorant,
the boy king distinctly odd? Had he
second thoughts about the Moor?

And was his stop-press dedication impassioned
or politic? *Sebastian, my King, Guarantor*
of our Ancient Liberties, born to extend
the Empire of the Faith ... (a case of poetry

making something happen? Disaster!)

3.

Summer long
on all the beaches, children
sculpture in sand
the Discoveries:

anchors, caravels,
Henry the Navigator,
Adamastor
of the Cape of Storms.

Summer long
on all the beaches, the sea
salt with tears of Portugal
swills them away.

4.

I'm still wondering about Camões, having
myself (to compare great things with small)
been seduced overseas by visions of home
as a place where matters were better organised

and returned to the grim reality. Thatcher
was not unlike Sebastian, and the Falklands
turned on a coin. Now we are hoist
with myths of greatness betrayed, and I recall

the honourable old man at Belém cursing, as
the caravels waited, *this lust for gold,
this ambition to be lords of India, Persia,
Arabia and Ethiopia, this cruel ferocity*

with its philosophy of death. Camões
invented him and gave him eloquence, but
the north wind swelled the sails (as it did)
and nothing could undo the vast event

(which the poet, as true historian, marvelled at).

5.

Pessoa wrote
in restaurants, alone
with his heteronyms
clamorous disquiet.

His bronze, in his beloved
Chiado, loiters
at a pavement table,
dipping its fountain pen in wine
as the estuary drifts.

(I've tried this in England:
people think I'm a policeman.)

6.

And here he's again, the Father
of Winds. Our matted pines
heave like an ocean, the almond trees

fuss prettily, ancient olives
munch and fumble, blue gums
bunch their shadow-boxing fists,

while up on the skyline, royal palms
semaphore with their ostrich feathers
to clouds scudding like clippers

on the Azores run. The Atlantic's
in every blast, and how
the swallows pinion it, cruising

under our block's cliff, accelerating
in the domestic air, hitting
the corner, and

FLAWEWEWEWEWE they are puffballs, ounces
of cartilage, sheer as silk to spattering
on the tessellated pavements,

feathering at the last split-
second in a teetering
pole-vault, swooping, skimming

the perfected charcoal of their shadows.
I watch them
trying on wings. I watch them

readying for the dangerous currents south.

Ruanda

The wine spreads on the tablecloth,
Bloodstains darken on the sand.
I do not want to look at these pictures
Which knock my heart and my hand
Spilling, as lives are spilt in that land.

It was country fat with leaves.
Beans and pawpaw jumped where you threw them.
Who could forget such serious smiles,
Such courtesies if once you knew them?
What gods have done this to them?

A freckled girl, her hair distracted,
Gestures to the milling refugees.
Somehow, it seems, she is responsible
For their flour and water. How can this be?
Has all this been done to flatter me?

At the heart of where we come from
Is the mark of what we are.
My hand scrubs at the wine stain,
My eyes turn from the horror
(Far downstream, the corpses drift ashore).

Red Alert

You, the scientist on the coconut
island with a bunker and flotsam
of lubricious girls, cloning
yourself to rule the earth;

you, the double-agent hurtling
down the corridor while explosions
mount to a fireball, the silkiest
blonde undulating in your arms;

you, the man at the traffic lights
waiting for green, you are far
madder, you with the supermarket
trolley, you with the pension.

The Instinct

1.

A third of a century ago I knew Lal,
a thin, brown man with high cheek bones
and evasive slits for eyes. For a while

we were friends, though with little in common
beyond Slim, his brother-in-law's steelband
which filled my days then, along with a woman

I had partly forgotten until I remembered Lal.
He was somehow special for being no one,
just Lal, no surname, jobless, no definable

Portuguese, Indian, Chinese or African
symptoms, just an end-of-line everyman
occupying earth. I met him once with a bin

of shoes he was trashing in the storm drain.
Neighbours had paid him to heel them. Ditching
the drumfull, he was ready to start again.

That's all I knew of how he made his living.
'Sometime,' he said of the shoeless, 'I does
really wonder if they know what they doin'.'

But in just one line of his life, hunched
over a tenor pan clawed from an oil drum
tempered in a furnace of tyres, its notes punched

out with a sawn-off six-inch nail, Lal
was the sweetest of perfectionists. No one
could double-wrist a purer, silkier drum roll,

more violin than percussion, from the piano-toned
ring of fifths round the pan's circumference,
nor beat from the off-pitch silver medallions

of the dustbin's shrill concave, tighter scales
or more intricate arpeggios in what he termed,
wryly as I arranged them, 'heavy classics'.

He brought, far more than me to this craft
of poetry, six hours nightly practice.
He was a man who taught me and, before I left,

I made him, along with Midnight, Wayne, Smokey,
Slim, Scorpion and the band, just one,
ambiguous gift, an American tour. Disembarked,

he vanished conclusively into that vacant heaven.

2.

Years afterwards, in another language,
in an African village so obscure
she had to borrow a wrap to meet me,
I met with Emily Makua.

Her wuthering name showed Britain
had some priestly hand in her past,
part redeeming, part embellishing
but abandoning her at last.

Even the cloth she borrowed
was a third-hand Java print.

She lived beyond the periphery
of where money's made and spent.

Approaching her was a *rite de passage:*
at the ford, discarding my shoes,
I was too soft to continue barefoot
(my companions couldn't choose).

She was wizened yet articulate,
a widow with nothing to hide.
She spoke of her eleven babies,
nine of whom had died.

Being Christian, she refused to talk
of witches, or blame her husband:
being respectful, she cast her life
in the third person plural of custom.

A sleeping mat, a pot, a ladle,
a corner of somebody's hut:
I had met no other human being
so utterly destitute.

I sat on the chair they brought me,
she knelt on the beaten mud floor.
I asked about maize, cotton, rubber, tobacco:
she wouldn't agree she was poor.

She repeated a story I had heard
inattentively elsewhere,
about a barren woman who coaxed and moulded
a baby from a cucumber.

When her neighbour's children ate it,
she was taken up to heaven
and offered two clay pots, one new,
still eddying from the oven,

the other cracked and blackened
by years of household fires:
she warmed to it, and from it leapt
the child of her desire.

Back home, her neighbour envied her:
heaven gave her equal treatment:
she chose the flawless pot and flames
consumed her on the instant.

Such tales have little resonance
when reported by my peers:
from such a person in such a place
it moved me to tears.

3.

These I write of were never my audience
(how could I hope to speak to them?)
but in fashioning experience

they became touchstones for a poetry
plain as an oil drum or cooking pot,
chastened by fact, scorning hyperbole

and all unreflecting metaphor, but an art
capable of such transformations
as the agile wrist or the heart's

yearning of those (never the 'other') reduced
to nothing or to no one, can kindle
summoning words and music.

I trusted on such evidence speech,
sure as whatever guides the swallow
or propels salmon to their home reach,

to keep us human, re-inventing
the aboriginal word made flesh
(with reference to our necessary closure).

Massamba with the Brilliant Flowers
(i.m. Luiza Drennon, 1924-91)

1. Alcabideche

After the mass in her memory when her daughters
Prayed for her journeying soul
In the village she knew only from their letters

To Africa, we gathered to eat the meal
She would have cooked for her sons-in-law,
Massa, massamba and, squatting by the charcoal

Brazier with a tumbler of smokey Portuguese *Dão*,
Two peppered chickens spiked like crucifixes,
Shrugging off with an indignant 'Chi-sá'

Any male offers of help as she licked
The knife and pronounced them done.
This was five thousand miles ago, a far cry

From the white-robed daughters of Zion
Singing of chariots swinging low, of the roll call
Yonder she had answered in heaven

With rest beyond Jordan for her ransomed soul.
These were the hymns of her comfortless years
Making one daughter a stranger at her funeral,

Weeping with the singers but preferring a mass
For the mother whose disappointments were catholic.
She died God's orphan, a cantankerous

Wanderer. She lost every trick
As power's colour changed round her. Every rule
She bent to – child marriage, the black

Face of poverty and labour – every accommodation failed
As her places failed her, leaving her
Grieving over the twins, divorced, with the rebels

On the city road and flight across the border
Her Rock of Ages refuge. So, after the blessing
Of the Host and the Benedictus, we gathered

Sadly with salt and maize flour for our own *massa*,
Pre-packed from the hypermarket on the *Marginale*,
And two chickens from the factory spiced

With her paste of lemon, pounded pepper and garlic,
With beers on ice, the charcoal tinkling,
The sons-in-law subservient to her liking,

And *massamba* begged from the *quinta*
In the dry lagoon of old Senhor Palmiro
Who was bemused by these exotics from Moçambique

Hovering like butterflies along his furrow,
Picking pumpkin leaves to be steamed with coconut,
With tomatoes, onions and the brilliant flowers,

And blossoming at the table in three of her daughters,
Each of them taller in unconscious mime,
Chafing in the households she had nurtured

And pilloried, bewitched and bewitching as her prime.

2. York

December's end. The kitchen half-door
swings open on the bulb-lit yard where
rain is drifting like firework
smoke, like the spray of a windblown

waterfall into our yellow
pond of lamplight. Below is a sprig
of mottled green-and-off-white
ivy, waxed like a tree frog.

Beyond, in the dark tank of moonless
starless midnight, sleek
buds of the flowering currant
are luminous as tropical fish.

So the year ends in blessedness,
a festering family quarrel
healed, a dear friend
resurrected from the living death

of the camps, the old words printed.
Out there, in the mild night under
soil under the fine rain,
tubers and roots stir quietly

of crocuses, cornflowers,
irises and blue geraniums,
tulips and nasturtiums,
lilies, foxgloves, the poppies' brilliant

unsteady silks,
reliable as night and day
with their calendar of beauty,
are out there, stirring

in the darkness
under the fine spray,
while she for whom we grieved
this year in the grim void

of her going, stirs
now in our hearts more calmly
with thoughts of her good
years, the satires we repeat

at table, lovingly, laughingly, sharing
her with our friends, bequeathing
pride to our half-listening
sons off-stage who,

barely remembering her, wear
her mark as we do. She swung
open my heart to simplicity
by her death with its quiet beginnings.

War Poem

The hundred hours of Desert Storm
I was watching my lawn
     for bulbs springing
(the rest is for those who were there).

There may be a time for requiem
or selfless eulogy in Arabic
     or possibly English,
but which of us will write them?

Our passionate craft (to cut
the diamond metaphor,
     ridicule all
courtiers, burnish the other

in ourselves) dwindled
when it broke
          on our screens,
shaming first person singulars.

These poems of yours,
sniffing fastidiously
     at soldiers'
argot, raping attention

with the very horrors they deplore,
they preen, they comply
     with violence:
you were none of you in any danger.

The seven days of Port Stanley
I was studying
     a village in Africa
(the rest is for those who were there).

Buddleia

From next door's patch the butterfly bush
is an indigo Niagara.

High above the purpling vine, it
thunders on our lake of michaelmas daisies,

and all hours of October daylight
painted ladies, tortoiseshells, cabbage whites, dashing red admirals

flock in flocks to its whirlpools.
At nightfall, when hawk moths mope and the swallows

have mutated to bats, they are
still there basking with the roaring in their ears, deaf

to the Minster's bells punching the night air.
It is an attitude to poetry and darkness.

Obituaries: Up an' Under

21 January, aged 43, Countess 'Titi' Wachtmeister
  6 February, aged 83, William Younger GC
Model and sometime companion to Peter Sellers
  Hero of the Louisa Colliery disaster when 19 men
Along with King Gustav and ex-Beatle George Harrison
  Died in the blast or from snorting firedamp
(Condemned as 'vulgar' by the Crown Estates office
  He was at the coal face with two fellow deputies
When he tried to re-name his nightclub 'Titi's'
  And before midnight explosions wracked the seam).

Titi, with the looks of a blonde Jean Shrimpton
  But Younger knew all the shafts and roadways
A successful cover girl when she burst on London
  And ignored danger, clambering to the scene through
Parties and diplomatic modelling and society balls
  Derailed tubs and galleries choked with dust
Where Ben Ekland, Brit's brother, introduced Titi
  His canary dead, his lamp glowing barely a foot,
To Sellers, still married to Lord Mancroft's daughter
  And wrestled with his colleagues for almost two hours
Igniting a passion, despite their age difference,
  To move the injured and dying to a safer drift
But it ended in a wrangle over a Cartier watch
  Enabling five miners to be stretchered to the surface
Along with Titi's jewels and a favourite stuffed dog.

Gossip predicted marriage to King Gustav, but Titi
  Awarded the George Cross for gallantry
Wed Enrico Monfrini, a Geneva-based corporate lawyer
  Younger, modest and self-depreciating
The wedding attracted 150 jet setters
  After almost half a century in the pits,
Including Gunter Sachs and Dai Llewellyn
  A grieving widower with two proud daughters
But a plumper Titi emerged from her separation
  Embodying the staunchness of the mining community
With a line of high-priced T shirts called 'T-T's Ts'
  (He bore his failing predicate with courage).

(adapted from *The Times*, 10 February, 1993)

Blueprint

(for Angus Calder)

I was born in 1940, the night of the fall of France,
My mother hated Churchill but my father wore the pants.
From my nappies I was short-changed on phlegm and nonchalance
But Nightingales sang, etc.

My memory's a blank slate till 1943.
By then, the tale was shatterproof, chalking out mystery,
But something in those blank days has inked its tread on me
We'll meet again, etc.

Dunkirk, the Blitz, the Spitfire few, my father had it pat,
Good and evil, black and white, Hamburg's tit-for-tat
(My mother would have hailed in blood a women's coup d'etat)
Run, rabbit, run, etc.

What happened between them when fire fell from the sky
I don't know, I'll never know, swaddled in my
Premature bottom drawer cot, with *Li-
lacs in the spring again*, etc.

Afterwards, my neckhair bristling at sirens, the sliver
-silver fuselage between cloud puffballs for once and ever
'That's Jerry' and balloons ears, afterwards or never
There'll be bluebirds over, etc.

Till the pathescope begins with Dave Waddell's Messerschmidt
(He called it an altimeter, he'd got it from an Austin)
Smuggled along the back row of 'Yield not to temptation',
Don't sit under the apple tree, etc.

And Joyce Hopkinson spiking her hand on the ARP barbed wire,
How we laughed at her shrieking, tugging at her knickers
Until crimson on her left elbow satisfied our anger,
  You'd be so nice to come home to, etc.

And with the child's sure instinct of dark things suppressed
(Was he truly erect in the Blitzkrieg's caress?
Did she openly exult with Armageddon at her breast?)
  Who do you think you are kidding? etc.

How could I live with such perfections of bereavement,
The righteous logic of Germany's bedevilment?
I longed for ambivalence as a honed achievement
  Lili Marlene, etc

Till a film from 'lands beyond the seas' kindled my qualms
With its tale of swamps and idolatry. Disbelief could blossom
With its feet in mangrove, its crown among the palms
  I've got a luverly bunch, etc.

I praised the cafe tables of a dust yard between frontiers,
The plank-and-oil-drum pontoons crossing rivers in the delta
The city on the sandbank with its conspiratorial poets
  Knock on wood, etc.

Till there came another war. It is waged by brutalised
Children. Some are just 12. They have mutilated
Or been forced to eat their parents. And they accumulate.
  If the sun should tumble from the sky, etc.

Letter to My Son

I am fifty years old
    and writing to you from high summer.
Wheat fields from the hollow
    to the swelling horizon
Have been combine-scythed
    in swirling parallel strokes.
There are swallows up here
    clicking in African languages.
Black cattle wading
    in the shadows of olive trees
Are barely visible
    so black are the shadow pools.
Cicadas among the cornflowers
    are sawing at their washboards
(A linking image from my '50s bored
    teens to your own, as

Suddenly articulate
    you start your own journey).
Whatever I can give you
    has long been given if at all.
There's little more you will
    draw on beyond occasional cheques.
But I want to write of my love
    for you over seventeen winters,
Both the barren anxiety
    that shadows your present choices,
And my pride in you
    and your emerging designs
Like a carnival of poppies
    crowding the disturbed soil
Of motorway embankments
    with their gift of summer.

Self-Praises

(for my African age-mates)

I climbed the old elm tree and read *William* books in the rook's nest,
My knee stuck in the pulpit rail: for once the congregation laughed,
The missionary told of the poison ordeal: I was spellbound in the cub hut,
I won the match by slicing a six off the back of the bat over backward point,
I cycled a hundred miles precisely to Nettlebed and back to town,
I planted crotons, a whole hedge in thirty-two varieties,
I scored Sparrow's *Melda* for the steelbands' *Panorama,*
I made love to the circuit-minister's wife in a dark corner of the canefield,
I decamped from the island under an arch of leaping dolphins,
Baboons jumped on my steaming bonnet as I stalled on the escarpment,
I crossed the longest bridge at dusk, reading of another country,
I found her on a sand dune where a coconut palm strained at its bole,
She to whom all metaphors return was outlined with chevrons,
She stretched like a tigress, adorned with her stripes,
I watched the Beetle spinning downstream, swept from the flooded causeway,
My dugout parted the hyacinths in search of the hidden history,
When the armed guerrillas ambushed us, I said *Oh, there you are,*
From four jobs I resigned,
From the fifth the President deported me, without rhyme or explanation,
I helped at my son's birth: he came out looking dumbfounded,
My proudest expedient, bribing our baby on to the plane!
The professor rang at midnight: my poem was a masterpiece,
I designed and built a kitchen to a millimetre's calculation,
I knuckled down to fifteen years of mortgages and pension,
I campaigned for my dear friend to step forth like Lazarus,
My vine, in Viking territory, was a miracle of survival,
My garden exploded in poppies and cornflowers: autumn blazed in

nasturtiums,

He wrote marvellously of his resurrection: it was I gave the writing space.
They shook hands, enemies to the vein,
They shook hands and reminisced across my conference table
(The student wrote: *thank you, who else could we have got drunk with?*).
As a scholar, I set the paradigm: as a poet I found my niche.
Let these praises float from my window, setting fires where they will.

Bacalhau

1.

Another restaurant in Alcabideche! People
keep asking, *where's the new restaurant?*
and Alice directs them
confidently without having seen it.

Restaurants in Alcabideche are like
chapels in Wales. There is always some
new delicate doctrine
involving fresh coriander and salt cod.

At Christ's birth, codfish loom
on our TVs, glottal as Pavarotti,
roaring *Hark the herald* etc.
(The turkeys wilt and swoon.)

2.

Bacalhau again! I found it
in Soho, but 'it comes
from Hull' said Luigi, his
moustache quivering

at the absurdity: 'they send
the heads to Portugal.'

I hugged it under my elbow,
a brown paper rugby ball
in a neat net of string,
and set off across London.

At the F.O.
they were bombing Libya.
'One moment, sir'.

'It's *bacalhau*,' I said.
'Sir?'
'Salt dry cod.'

Gingerly, he weighed the device,
gave it a gentle wobble,
smelt it and held it to his ear
listening to the music of the seas.

'Salt. Dry. Cod, sir?'
'They send the heads to Portugal
under the Treaty of Windsor'.

He kissed the air and a dog,
special breed, tall
as the hat stand ambled
from the office, taking control.

My casket was offered knee high
like myrrh or frankincense
and I thought of the hundred recipes
simmering in the brown egg

- bacalhau
  in the glorious names
of Bulhão Pato, Gomes de Sá,
Batalha Reis, António Lemos,
Zé do Pipo and Brás.
  - bacalhau
    with cheese, with onions,
  with potatoes and spinach,
  with milk, rice, leeks, oysters,
  parsley, prawns, flour with egg white
  - bacalhau 'with everything'
    in the peasant style
with carrots
in the manner of heaven,
in twists like a corkscrew,
from Trás os Montes
  Guarda, Porto,
    Lamego,
      Ericeira,
        Alentejana, even
the despoiled Algarve,
and our winter favourite
  - bacalhau que nunca chega,
    'the cod that's never enough' –

I watched them hatching in the dog's
nostrils, clamouring
to spawn in the cold seas
of their birth.
          (Ghadafi'd
have surrendered on the instant,
adding his own touch
of tabina and walnuts.)

108

The Alsation took a quarter sniff
turning its tail contemptuously.
Cook, poet, comedian,
I was harmless.
Our government's in safe paws.

(Alice White faults this poem for not including *Bacalhau á moda
da Guida*, as prepared by Margarida Maria da Cruz Mergulhão
of Casal Verde, Figueira da Foz.)

Update from a Distant Friend
(Zomba to Blantyre, after Jan Kees Van Donge)

'Their uniforms were new to me, shimmering
Pink and purple, and so was their elation.
At the hospital stop they commandeered
The all-but-empty bus and I thought them
Kitchen orderlies or the like from, maybe,
Thondwe, but we humped the bridge
Luminous at dusk and they stayed on board
Joking like people with an explosive secret.

'Night fell and we clattered the tarmac
In our yellow tunnel between darkness
And the blue gums. The furred hills
To the west bristled against the sky's
Slashed purple and pink, and every
Five kilometres or so an estate house
Radiated wealth in this land of silenced
Villages. At the Magomero turn-off

'I was drawn with my halting chiChewa
Into their talk. Who were they? Where
Were they going? This fired guffaws
And head-wagging with a mutual
Slapping of palms, and this riddle:
Who travels without travelling to?
Slave who's impregnated the chief's
Wife! Hunter with buffalo in his path!

'At Njuli, they'd a new one for me:
Who counts up instead of counting down?
We reached the firelit shacks of the first
Squatter camps, then the first township,
And I tried to imagine these landless people
Mounting instead of sliding. But I was
In the wrong market. *It's the detainee,*
They told me, *not the sentenced prisoner.*

'And that was their tale. Freed that day
To honour the Dictator's brain surgery,
Held while the unlucky rioted (two dead),
Then smuggled out in their pink and purple.
The man sharing my seat had done 24 years.
When we reached the depot with no onward
Buses that night, I was emotionally
Broken at the gap between their lives and mine.'

Xmas Dinner

Our recipe starts ruthlessly, *Mata-se*
O leitão (kill the piglet) *com um golpe*
Na goela (with a sharp blow to the throat)!
All feasts begins with a death, but who capable

Of doing this needs to read how to do it?
And which of us ex-patriates could accomplish
Such an act? Could pretty Odette
(Who wrote our cookbook) do it? Does she

Require it of her husband? This is no
Recipe, but an elegy for a vanished
Portugal. Picture, it tells us, the tiny
Backyard in the cobbled street of whitewashed

Cottages, among the pruned vineyards
Of Bairrada, where the piglet you feast on
Was bred at your hands, and manhood
Knows what's its due and what's due to woman.

Odette concludes, *Borrifa-se* (use a spray
Of parsley) to sprinkle the piglet
Generously with white wine. So picture me,
Kneeling on the kitchen floor, attempting it.

The Most Deceiving

Fernão Mendes Pinto. Viva!
memorialised in the famed *Thesaurus*
as *conjurer, deceiver, liar,*
trickster, humbug, a massed chorus

of *Pharisee, Rosicrucian, Jesuit,*
actor, jobber, dissembler, charlatan,
all because you refused to credit
the Portuguese could civilise Japan!

In your book, the pious Catholic
pirate, ruthless as any infidel,
bound by his imperial ethic
rapes, despoils, betrays, kills.

You mock yourself as God's missionary
lampooned for eating with your hands.
How could you not go down in history
but as by-word for the *soi-disant?*

Medicaster, saltimbanco,
I hope in Dante's whichever hell
jockey, perjurer, Cagliostro
Roget's doing time for libel.

My question's this: as you ploughed
old memories into your jeremiad
blockbuster *Perigrinação*,
did you know of C. and his *Lusíads?*

While the picaresque and satiric
danced from your goosequill in Almada,
the sublime and truly epic
went begging in Alcântara,

the briefest of river trips apart,
within hailing distance as it were.
Did you never share a heart-to-heart
with that other Eastern warrior?

Your buccaneers were his *barões*.
He saw God's designs turning
on the deeds of mariners you disowned
and reckoned fit for burning.

Two masterpieces, alternate visions,
divided by an estuary
which drifts into the setting sun,
that uncompromising referee.

You won your case, you lost your cause,
for history's unkind to truth,
bestowing all her best applause
on those capable of myth.

It's no unflattering epitaph
to be yoked with the most deceiving,
Luís de Camões' apocryph,
and an author to believe in.

October's Sickle Moon
(for Abu Zeide Mohamede Ibne Mucana)

*(The pull of the soil was always very strong for the Andalusian
poets who, for the most part, were of country origin ... Such was
the case of Ibne Mucana al-Isbuni. Having lived at Seville at the
court of the Abbadides, then at Granada at the court of Zirides,
he knew the inanities of the courtier's life and relinquishing the
bogus fame of the royal salons he returned to his village of
Alcabideche, close by Sintra, to end his life cultivating his field.
'I saw him' said one of his fellow countrymen who recounted to
Ibne Bassam his encounter with the old poet, now deaf, his sickle
in his hand. 'I approached him and when I had taken him by the
hand he made me sit down to look at the field ... I asked him to
recite some poetry and he improvised.')*

1.

'Dwellers at al-Qabdaq, husband well your seeds
          whether of onions or pumpkins.
A man of purpose needs a windmill turning
          with the clouds, not with water.
Al-Qabdaq doesn't produce, even in a good year,
          more than twenty sacks of corn.
Any more than that, the wild pigs come down
          from the forest in regular armies.
She is meagre with anything good or useful,
          just like me, as you know, I have a poor ear.
I abandoned the kings in their finery, I refused
          to attend their processions and parted from them.
Here you find me at al-Qabdaq, harvesting thorns
          with my sharp and agile sickle.
If someone said, 'Is it worth this trouble?'

you'd answer, 'The noble man's ensign is freedom'.
Abu Bakr al-Muzaffar's love and good deeds were my guide
    so that I left for a garden in springtime.'

2.

We meet the old deaf poet with a sickle, crofting
The northern border of a country whose south
Is the River Senegal. He has turned his back on
Kings in their finery, comparing men of purpose
With windmills, circling with the clouds, not
Water – though we may be sure these rains, after
The scorched weeks of house-repairs and weddings,
This season of the pumpkin and onion seeds he
Celebrates in his poem, when olives ripen and lamplike
Oranges burnish the quick dusk at the Call to Prayers,
We may be sure October's crocuses are a sign.

He lives when the Straits open on nowhere, perilous
To sailors pitched west in the inland sea but
No border. After the drought, October's rains.
Then the winds blow from Guinea and heat returns.
For him, this is Morocco and ordinary. The world
Is neither Europe nor Africa. These slopes of heather
And copper bracken, these drifting wine-coloured
Leaves as the swallows gather on whatever in his
World are telephone wires, they speak of the rains.
Then the golden windfall oranges tumble among
Daffodils, signalling harvest and another season

Building families. He has two fears: the wild boars
From Sintra mountain, foraging through his corn
In packs, and Portugal, the kaffir north. Rightly,

For we came and took purchase. Today, after
Autumn's virginal crocuses and the swallows' flight
South, our chestnuts blaze every colour of Fall.
We have baptised his seasons (*Por São Martinho,*
Prova teu vinho), and ceased believing. Our cliffs
Bristle with immigration patrols. His stone windmills
Are chic retirement homes for the circling rich.

Yet dawn brings walls of morning glory, houses
Shining at jigsaw angles, the oliveira's feather-
Light windmill, the church on the mound where
Water, which explains all, still springs from the rock.
All day our houses soak up sun, surrendering
Colour, storing heat in a stunned precision of light
And shade. Over-exposed, even the windmill falters.
Beyond everything, the Atlantic's razor blade.
Our dusks are green wine. In the windmill's spinning
Penumbra, olive trees smoulder. Houses blaze
Separate textures. The dry-stone cabbage allotments

Glow like skylights, where we encounter the old
Poet extemporising in strict metre his satires
On the wretched soil of his birthplace. He has
Abandoned processing with kings. He has brought
To this onion patch Aristotle and Galen, turning
At each line's end to complete the couplet.
He husbands seeds. He grinds with the wind,
Spinning the cog-wheeled poetry of his freedom
In this all-man's-land, neither Europe nor Africa.
Tonight, as October's sickle moon sprints
Through marbled rain clouds, his windmills sigh.

Let me tell you, Jack ...

(for, and after Jack Mapanje)

Let me tell you, Jack, what's beyond the veranda
Where I write most days, except when the north wind
Blasts from York across Biscay to ravage
Our pottery garden of the plants you know from home
- Hibiscus, elephant ears, Mary's milk, *piri-piri*.

I've lost count of the half poems launched to probe
For metaphors to enshrine what's out there. *Enshrine!*
Don't giggle! Obsolete words, like *enamelled*
Or *the painter's palette*, invade them for colours no one
Younger than 50 in England has ever exclaimed at,

And you know well enough I don't just observe
From a height. I'm down there daily, like Wordsworth
In the gap between stanzas, peering short-sightedly
At silks thrusting from the earth, and interrogating
Passers-by for the word, though they often don't know.

So my diary is of distances, of fragments and hesitations,
About white walls daubed with laundry and geraniums,
About the moss-green valley, where nettles even in winter
Surge knee-high, and snakes fat as pythons coil in the sun.
Pine trees cast shadows blacker than Alentejo bulls,

And spring's sequence of flowers is like a carpet somehow
Lit from within, changing not by the month or the week
But hourly between daybreak and noon and dusk
As the massed gold or china-blue or tortoiseshell petals
Open, revolving with the blossoming sun, and fold and decline.

I watch the cat boxing her kittens. Boys yelp like peacocks.
Cocorico happens too often to be any use as a clock.
Oh, but laugh at this! Our morning parade, as housedogs
Walk their mistresses, each circumscribed by her territory
Marked by a tree, a lamppost, and a raised hind leg.

You would hardly know the Atlantic is just a kilometre
Off, until the stump of a hurricane howls from New York
And the rain clouds scud like caravels, their hulls
Careened by the moon. Skies are important here, stars
In their consternations, flagging imperial destinies,

So I use you as reference point, your well being differently
Based, knowing our love (another jaded word, with its
Dangerous afterlife) will survive this latest exchange
Of countries and poems. This valley beyond my veranda
Is my newest mystery, my second-hand Brazil,

Where I'm less ex-patriate than in York. Out there
Between the almond trees and blue-black cypresses
Is a field of flowers where the Angolans are playing football.
Language will come. I want to continue living
Where I will always marvel at precisely where I am living.

From
Traveller's Palm
(2002)

Where the Land Ends and the Sea Begins

1

On this headland of middle age and Europe
where the land ends and the sea begins
I write. October's rains are here.
Cicadas are shrilling in the pine trees,

and though swallows reckon this is autumn,
people are trooping to their allotments
with their Moorish over-the-shoulder hoes
to unlock the earth after the long drought,

and to one who, like Rilke, writes to correct
the mere accident of where I was born,
it's a swallow's instinct to resume
riding the waves of this place and time,

taking off from the edge, the gene
that propelled me half way round the world
to my mestiço muse, forging an idiom
in contradiction, from antipodes.

4

In front of the train's front seats, next
to the driver's cabin, with the same view,
is a fold down seat we evening commuters
jostle for, like school boys. Ours

is the fast train, skirting the estuary
the whole track to where the sun sinks
in the ocean. So close to the crashing
breakers is our tilt, the windows

crust with salt. Beach after beach
we see waders in their tribal feather.
The little boats and the golden girls
seem each man to his dream accessible,

though as eloquent are the Hornby points,
the rails' narrowing script, turned
Arabic by the spume. I sense this
journey plunging me back. And onwards.

6

Ridiculous, a year this side of sixty
to be sitting on the veranda over the garage
worrying she is an hour late, as though
I were still twenty with a teenager's

tangle of emotions and a young husband's pride.
But dusk is closing on our customary sun-downer
and my hearts kicks at the thought of the message
that must one day far too early come

about her to me or about me to her
in no pidgin I will understand or signs
in any way bearable. I know from its vowels
that is not our Rover rounding the corner

nor her whine of deceleration, yet I stare
down all the same just as the phone screams
and it's okay, she's at her sister's, yes of course,
until ten, of course, yes, everything's fine.

7

He was on furlough, back from Africa,
back to winter in the blacked-out
cub hut with our cropped heads and carbolic
knees, the gas-heaters puckering,

and his tale was of idolatry. Spell-
bound. we swallowed the poison ordeal.
Today, I know how zestfully those
mission girls hammed it, squealing

at the witchdoctor's bones and fly whisk
and slavering at his feet. The pathescope
made Akela fret. She trusted magic
lanterns, not his silver flickering

like Jane Russell 'being photographed'.
Our missionary egged us to scoff.
I did. But secretly I saw. Those blackies
knew something. Out there was life.

9

In dusty tomes at the back of livrarias
or on tiles in the loveliest of the old palaces,
they are still there, the Three Graces,
Portuguese, Indian and Brazilian Negress,

embracing or in triptych, each displaying
all but one of her charms and proffering
gifts, the apple, the mango, the pawpaw,
while around them curve the appropriate

fronds of banana, palm and olive branch.
They celebrate possession, the fruitfulness
of a bankrupt empire. They are three Eves
with the appropriate serpents, Man's fate

on three continents. But who is not charmed
by their sisterhood? Each is different
but perfect. They let us dream innocently
of universal love (at least among womankind).

The Trick

10

The week I landed, I couldn't distinguish
face from face, tree from tree. I found
girls too ripe, the flowers over-doing it,
the sunsets vulgarly ostentatious,

and the night sky, in dazzling 3D
with its billion lamps, intimidated.
How could I read such over-statement
when irony withered on the tongue?

Beissel described priapic breadfruit,
hibiscus with their flies undone. Witty,
of course, but false. The trick
was never to adumbrate the exotic,

but to be re-born, writing as though
such miracles were entirely natural,
the scheme of things. As began to happen
when faces cracked into separate smiles.

13

It was Scorpion told me limbo dancers
was either Pepsi or Coke. He doubled
as fire-eater ('Don't ever breat' in',
he warned), and dancer on broken glass.

One Sunday practice he came up the trace
limping, his heel bandaged. 'A bottle
cut it right here in my yard'. Five Past,
who did striptease, laughed (she was blacker

than her twin who was born at midnight).
'On stage,' he said. 'dey does heap it up'.
It gave Lord Keskidee, our calypsonian,
his road march. But he missed the joke

of me on bass, doubling as impresario
to the Augustans and late Romantics
(memo: Pepsi/Coke bottles measured the depth
of the latest rod they had to limbo under).

14

To us once Baptists, linked in the priesthood
of non-believers, confession's denied.
Should I write *My Wicked, Wicked Life*
assured of credence and absolution? No,

guilt's what you refuse to speak of, lives
you brushed like a bat's wing ominously,
or left in the shark's shadow, for motives
irreconcilable with what you teach your sons.

Observe! I'm at it too, bearing my breast,
wearing my heart on the sleeve I use
to wipe my face of crocodile tears. Your poet's
fallible, it says, paradoxically true!

There was one ritual we had: testimony,
the fiction of how we encountered Jesus.
After came the plunge, dying to rise
again. Another language, a changed life.

18

For better or worse, too late for my marriage,
it was where I became a man. I found
things to say people noted, without irony's
evasions. By night my music prospered.

For richer, for poorer, I found my first
book, and the sensuous joy of dry enquiry
in smacked tomes, the dust glinting as
jingles blazed through the library window.

In sickness and in health, I found I could
betray, and failure be like celebration
in sweet assignations, the half-furled
curtain flaunting her husband's absence.

Till death us depart, I learned to quit
in a parody of baptism, striding
across the steaming tarmac, my shadow
dancing before me like a freed prisoner.

19

Each full moon, swimming at dusk
above the ridge where dawn
dawns, is a reckoning. How
has your month been spent?

Its red, quizzical face questions
intimately. What are you about?
Where are the poems you could have written?
How many hours have you given to love?

It peers like a Chinese grandmother
cracking her knuckles. What have you
done for your children? To which
ancestors have you poured wine?

Each desert, earth-bound moon,
tilting in the sun's reflected
light, asks, Where in the world
are you going? There is no other.

The New Smiling Bwanas

20

Dawn hung like dripping sailcloth
over the plumed reeds and papyrus. Tiny
crocodiles as I came in deck plopped
overboard and dissolved. Mosquitoes

drifted like an English drizzle. The barge
swivelled, scouring a bend into a gold
column on the sliding eddies. Then
heat whipped all colours into hiding.

Three days we chugged between countries
emblematically left and right, though the women
gesturing port and starboard their satiric
invitations wore the same embossed bras

and the houses sprouting like grey mushrooms
in the hut-high millet were identical.
Traveller's tales. The girl relaxed in the stern
reading Austen's *Orgulho e Preconceito*.

21

Mwandiona pe, the Shona name, *from where
did you see me?* assumes the vanished
bushmen are playing hide and seek.
On that bald dome of gneiss balancing

impossible boulders four high on its forehead,
much could be believed. We climbed

higher and saw springbok and impala
leaping across the cave wall like a movie,

and a shambling elephant, and buffaloes
keening the air, for all the skill
of the stick-figure hunters, poised.
As we descended, the chartered valley

creased by its turquoise river seemed empty
 - though not to Dambushawa, who knew
from every crack and dry water course
playful spirits peered and were chuckling.

24

Jack's was about a butterfly bar girl
who saddened him, being (in his poem)
from Kadango. At his navel-name
greeting, she floated to the next customer.

Lupengah's villagers were dismayed.
In their rain dance, the lightening cock struck
Beauty, charring her waist beads. *I'll
find out*, said the chief, solemn and grieved.

'Up at Katoro you see the red sky'
wrote exiled Scopas, dreaming
of his beloved Juba Town, its ashes
that stood like anthills under napalm.

Late in the night of our first safari
to tickle the censors of that Banda-stan,
my own was tabled: the chief's daughter
dancing to *The Seekers* outside her hut.

26

For these roadside markets we always
pull in. The sugar cane, maize cobs, sweet
potatoes, a brown paper twist of groundnuts,
cost nothing. But it isn't the money.

It's the living shadow, the neat pyramids
of colour, the peacock women, the courtesies
of purchase. As they tuck our small change
under their mats, our dust cloud settles.

Once, exhausted by the dirt road's
corrugations, we parked in a mango tree's
black disc. From the tall grass came
a woman, hoe on her forehead,

child on her back. She crossed
the road like a minefield, and into
the grass opposite, pursuing her
own journey at a tangent. Or we were.

28

What lion spits out, Jack said, *must be tough*.
I was flattered. Afterwards, on the VC10
banking north-east over the brimming river,
I saw it in different light as wise counsel.

Once from a dugout on that swift, pewter
river, I watched the slim jet tilting north.
Banished, I stared down at the boababs:
where snake suns himself must be comfortable.

A country of passive verbs. Deported
(my 48 hours sentence) or detained
(Felix was the first of our group to rot):
when hippo yawns, the pool dries up a little.

Taban was brusque, Okot pre-occupied
with harsher wrongs. It was re-resurrected
Ngugi who talked me through my pain
(active voices, *A Grain of Wheat*).

29

On the sultriest of days, even in August,
there will drift in from the white Atlantic
an invisible iceberg, blanking us
in a snow-queen's veil, like a cataract

over the pupils, or the touch of death's
palsy. At such moments, shivering
in my summer cottons, poetry's
empiricism matters, and like Shaka Zulu

shooting flaming arrows at the sun's
eclipse to restore his eddying thorn trees,
I begin writing furiously, conjuring
rhythm's steady feet as, sure enough,

the mist eases inland and dissolves.
Do they find us or we our metaphors?
I coin words from the instinct to survive,
well aware some evening the trick must fail.

There

31

They walk the city wall the seasons
round. The wall rounds the city. On that
light room, first floor, of morning sun
and sunset, we had purchase. Our

warm brickwork soaked up sun, baked earth,
a mud house really. So many crumbling
colours. Each brick, warm as an egg,
stored sunlight like a battery. But

the gathering wall the travellers walk
is limestone. Minster, Woolworths,
Swinegate and Wharf, it accommodates
the city. Walk, and you hold a halo

in your palm. In the damp gold of leaves
it glows at dusk the colour of owls
we out-stared at plane tree level. So,
walker, after all your ironies, autumn.

32

Our marriage spirals from the page (name
me a poet who bowed to his muse's
grandmother - or cousins, not to mention
sisters who, in the custom of her people,

could have been my wives too) which
is where our lovers' leap defies gravity,
for when Drennon, the Demararan, followed
the Indian grandfather from Mauritius,

taking the younger sister to breed an heir,
a helix sprang which can't be boxed
in those grids with a man at the apex. All
continued marrying outwards. Her genes

encompass history and continents
in a luminous web in which are charmed
men with whom I have nothing in common
beyond our drinking together at weddings.

33

Mid-May, Dafydd ap Gwilym's
month, and burning (hot air
from Africa, say the weathermen).
In the duckegg sky's a haze

of midges. We sunbathe by the late
tulips on our towel of lawn,
watching starlings pretending
to be swallows. Their lumpy

forages are laughable. They launch
swoops and abort them
in fluttering panic. They all-but
crash like dodgems. Suddenly,

two curved blades skim the eggshell
dome of our retinas in an intricate,
dizzying ice-dance. At last,
summer! The professionals are here.

34

Leaning over the banisters she could
watch him through the cellar window,
mashing, sparging, drawing off the wort:
male play, like rugby. But he made

home his centre. Whatever he brewed
of fitted cupboards or draught
excluders was for love. The bedroom
was snug, the lampshades pink.

Leaning over the banisters she feared
what fermented in the cellar of this
building she nannied in daily,
let out for weekend shopping. And he,

too, hated office. Money could not
redeem the month. As under the staircase
yeast sang, he
drank in the bitter of their passion.

38

Fool, look in thy heart and write?
I've always preferred what's out there
(perceiving, yes, my angle of vision's
a problem, I'm no naïve Platonist),

but let's examine this heart business.
To begin with, how for sure do you
know it's there? I unbutton my shirt
and probe beneath my left nipple,

or above it, or a little to the right -
- dammit, the thing's not even
beating, it's my wrist reassures me,
feel it on the pulse, said Keats,

and that's closer to the bone for me,
who always needed the external
doorways, only afterwards discerning
from the poem the matter in my heart.

39

Around the island in the midday glare
a dozen sooty cormorants drift.
They never alight. At times, one plunges
without creasing the estuary's mirror,

and ascends, vanishing at cliff height, where
above the loaf-shaped island in the heat
a dozen white gannets spiral. You
can barely see them, until one veers

and sunlight glints on its bright plumage
as its twin plunges. For there are no
cormorants, only the gannets' shadows
wheeling in the noon's distraction.

What labours within the green inlet
will never mate with the flopping heron.
The swallow skimming the River Douro
leaves its image dissolving as it soars.

Sinking Fund

43

Someone said you could buy chicken manure
in the hills, above Charlotte and Waterloo,
so I drove with Jalloh, sackcloth and a spade,
bumping the tarmac through the rain forest

where the orchids I wanted to grow grew
wild and chimpanzees, strap-
hanging above us, hooted insults
at my Imp. Climbing, we surfaced

at a twilit clearing. As promised, it was dirt
cheap. My spade was redundant as Mamadu
took charge. I asked Jalloh, 'How'd you
fancy living up here?' 'It far,' he muttered.

Mamadu, shovelling shit, straightened.
'Far?' he exclaimed. 'From WHERE?'
That raw pastoral has remained with me.
A cock crowed. The sun dropped on the instant.

47

Studiously, the villagers misled. For an hour
they kept us circling, until someone pointed
and I parked in a grass-walled compound.
Three huts. Flour bags. A thatched dormitory.

The woman rinsing uniforms in the corner
ignored us as Alice prepared Martin's bottle.
I was spreading the roadmap on our 127's
bonnet when a dozen armed guerrillas

sprang from ambush. 'Oh, there you are', I said,
smiling at the circle of Kalashnikovs.
Long afterwards, Rafael told me it was
the baby proved us harmless. At the time,

this all seemed normal. The commandant
gave me a letter: *The bearer* (of such idiot
nonchalance) *is a friend and wherever
he goes we request he should be well-treated.*

49

They knocked at midnight. Trustfully, I opened.
There is no speaking of the event, only
the aftermath. We clung together, singing
under the hostel Christmas tree, and I wrote

in foursquare reckoning of napalm
rained on innocents queuing for flour
in the camps they'd escaped from – that horror
eclipsing mine. And my wife's. And our child's.

Safe inside the stockade wall, for months
into years I knee-capped one with an axe,
flung boiling saucepans at another's face,
punctured their eyeballs with a garden fork

till with birdsong, trust returned. Under
a sky shaken by bells I grew back
into myself, watching our two sons flourish
(at times, Alice wakes at midnight, sobbing).

50

The ivory lion stalks the shelf,
the cat in the conservatory
claws at the vine, and for myself
what's out there is obligatory.

The massacres that never happened,
my own blood on the knotted floor
as, peddling their weaponry,
the great powers waged their proxy war.

Then, when the cave revealed its hoard
of rib and skull and musket barrel,
the deportation of the dead
defined the programme of my quarrel:

the base is time, the superstructure
bone and flesh and human guilt:
all our histories will fracture
in the cunning of that fault.

The Simplicity of Mountains

51

The last, mournful Arab in Obidos
is an Englishman, a contract manager,
in love with Portugal but, above all
else, admiring things properly run.

as when the Moors managed the Lagoa
as a seaway, right to the citadel's
western precipice, a shimmering
haven (as he will conjure it for you)

scything inland, matching beauty
with purpose, every centimetre farmed
for eels and oranges, corn and olive oil,
and governed by experts with eyes alert

to the brown silt descending the rivers
and the sand bar's linked architecture:
the citric, dawn wail of the muezzin,
the poetry of water, sun and rock.

53

The old king's ancestors established the kingdom
which the old king governed for sixty-two years.
Now the prince is in the forest, proving himself
with a hunt no living courtier has experienced.

This isn't like the casino or the girls drawing
Afrikaners in for forbidden relaxations,
nor is it done to placate the asbestos barons
who take their cut whatever the locals get up to.

Even the royalist paper is bemused, picturing
the First Minister gasping to maintain his urbanity.
At the university there are other girls. Their talk
is of labour value and surplus extraction. They

have no ambition to be hostesses, or royal wives.
Though the forest is a stricter school
than his Dorset 6th form, the teenage king
may soon be longing for the simplicity of mountains.

54

Xintra: the bleak ramparts on the summit,
keening the Atlantic and the northern plain,
must have been to the Moors like Hadrian's Wall,
the fog-bound palisades of an empire

whose green frontier was the Senegal River.
From this vertiginous forest, wild boars
raided, ravaging vineyards and fouling
wells. To the north, kaffirs threatened.

Reversed, the ramparts stared south
beyond the Tagus. For Luís de Camões'
ocean crusaders, nymph-haunted
Cintra was their last glimpse of the loved land.

With Byron it grew gothic, and a dull queen
turned the summit dungeons and dragons.
Today's Sintra has never been so crowded
with the seekers after solitude and the authentic.

55

All day the *impi* have been filing past the hotel.
They wear beadwork and brandish knobkerries.
They bear poles for the new king's cattle byre.
His krall is bedecked with shields and feathers.

From all over the kingdom they have carried their branches
and the cattle byre, when the regiments
dance there, will be perfect with the gift
of every town and village in the nation.

Cattle are the nation's wealth, held in trust
by the king. Cattle are currency. With cattle
you can purchase wombs, breed warriors,
double your herds with booty, only

then came the Gatling gun. Safe within
its compromises, this kingdom has forgotten.
The prince, who wields his knobkerry unconvincingly,
follows a different history. Or is possibly lost.

58

Ourique on its eminence, that hot November
Sunday, seemed abandoned. We looked outwards.
On the parched plain to the horizon, each
cork oak loitered in its pool of shadow.

Back in the square an old man rose, drank
from the fountain, and sat without turning.
Empty alleyways, their cobbles polished
to pewter, zig-zagged steeply to the church

past the town hall where Camões's chiselled
octavos told of the battle that possibly
was fought here with a list of the heroes
who perhaps won. My whisper, translating

this, rattled like grapeshot. An orange
dropped audibly, rolling in its gold foil
all the way down to the new by-pass,
though only we were around to record it.

60

The Helen of my verse has four tongues:
last, convent English, a dialect of rank
and baffling insinuations. My bald
syntax, laced with irony, freezes.

We met in chiNyanja, the dictator's
brogue, dangerous for lovers, when a kiss
could land you in Kanjedza. The sounds
of silence, whispered behind closed doors.

Her schooling was Portuguese. It made her,
ran the myth, civilised. It turned her,
burgeoned the fact, rebellious. A lingo
to stand no nonsense, not least from husbands.

But hear her in chiSena, her mother's
creole, knees spread, elbows akimbo,
her lips curled in fertile obscenities,
earthed, lacking only a pipe!

Special Delivery

61

Autumn, I breakfast with the bees
up here not for the flowers but the sun.
An hour after dawn, it breaks
hot and gold above the ridge opposite,

descending our boxed verandas
like a blow torch, and the bees hover
in full orchestra on invisible threads
of air, as mist burns off in the valley,

Then the dancing begins, in dizzying
spirals of ecstasy. I sit motionless,
breath suspended as three alight
on my arm and forehead, combing

their legs, then off again in helter-
skelters of frenzy. It's done, before
my coffee has cooled. They depart
without deflowering my felicias.

62

The doorbell rang. It was Jack, shorn
of his obituaries. I was dumb
with joy and Alice, hearing nothing, heard
something and rushed to embrace him.

After our tears, talk. There was money
and god, how proud I was there was money
and place. Beyond politics, beyond truth,
there was sanctuary for this driven family,

and my walk-on part in the dictator's fall
was ending with something done. I continued
as doorman-cum-secretary, harrowed
by glimpses of what I dimly guessed at,

bringing English insouciance to the abyss,
until one afternoon, two months on, I
passed him parked in a lay-by, scribbling
his first post-prison poem. And knew triumph.

64

My hunt's for the found poem,
the one that finds me, and not
in a book or newspaper, its words
already bolted into place, but

out there in what really occurs
to us or me or them, so instantly
a birth happens like a new bud
on the moonflower, or over time

a pattern flickers like candleflies,
and in creating just what took place
so even the Fiat's number plate
is unchanged, my job's to find

a style so transparent you don't
hear any voice of mine shouting
Look at Me, just the depths gleaming
without a ripple to refract the art.

67

In your absence the old angers burn.
Twenty-seven years have much to answer for.
Infidelities, buried when you are here,
howl desolately in the half double-bed

and I exhume the forgotten negatives
 - the absolute breach I could have preferred,
the others I could have preferred, leaving you
lying sweetly in the sheets of your choice.

Marriage is an endless affirmation
or it's nothing, and that nothing's
pride, and my lifelong pride's in you
or in nothing. Come, lover, come,

you've no truer friend where you are
or anywhere. It's summer. The charcoal's
caught and clinking. What's
your appointment? Come, lover, come.

68

Absent each February, I've missed
hoop-petticoat daffodils, all trumpet
with tiny spiked skirts, and mountain
rosemary, ship's hawsers flowering

in chalk blue butterflies, and the first
poppies, I don't believe it, wherever
bulldozers scarred the earth last spring
they're venturing their unsteady silks,

and everywhere, gold sorrel. How many
zillion *azedinhas* has Portugal? Imagine
some Salazar decreeing, 'Root out
all sorrel!' What madness! They gild

meadows and pruned vineyards, sprouting
from lampposts and stone walls, floating
up to ninth floor verandas, irrepressible
canaries, chirping the least glimpse of sun.

New Poems

Casa Uhuru

Flywell Ntima of that forgotten generation
for whom Pan Africanism would redeem
the world, has brought his wound
to a small estate, here in the Alentejo,

and stubbornly named it *Casa Uhuru*.
We have much in common, he and I, though
the same history scuppered my chances
of being a kindly DC on perpetual safari,

or a folklore crazed missionary. Our journeys
have brought us to plots in Portugal
in a pretence of putting down roots where race
is not too much of an issue. Our difference

lies in his greater ambition – viz., the flecked
bamboo he smuggled from the Ivory Coast
and watches like a nurse, or the evening
his French wife phoned him in Nairobi

to say the fever tree was in fresh shoot, and he
spent the whole night tossing in excitement.
As for his baobabs, he has three in pots,
stunted like bonsai, but in tiny leaf.

Imagine a savannah trembling with thorn trees,
a black mountain, cut by a highway,
where the poor have access and the educated prosper.
His *Casa Uhuru*'s a dream this dreamer's lost.

Stanzas to the Slave, Barbara

(from the Portuguese of Luís de Camões)

This slave I own
Who holds me captive,
Living for her alone
Who scorns to live,
I never saw woven
In bright bouquets
One dog rose lovelier
To my gaze.

The flowers in the field,
And the stars above
In their beauty, yield
To my love.
Distinct in feature,
Eyes dark and at rest,
Tired creature,
But not of conquest.

Here dwells the sweetness
By which I live,
She being mistress
Of whom she is captive.
Her hair is raven,
And the fashion responds,
Forgetting its given
Preference for blonde.

Love being Negro,
At so sweet a figure
The blanketing snow
Vows to change colour.

Gladly obedient
And naturally clever,
This may be expedient,
But barbarous, never!

Quiet presence
That silences storms,
All my disturbance
Finds peace in her arms.
This is the vassal
Who makes me her slave,
Being the muscle
That keeps me alive.

The Brown Girl

When, on the molasses barge reading Austen's
Orgulho e Preconceito, she was even then,
in the swamplands, plotting houses on envelopes,

Reader, we begin this poem a long way
back, with the brown girl, just twenty-one,
on a flooded tributary of the green Zambesi,

sketching rooms for family, for sleeping
and cooking, and a hatchet-hewn
fig wood table, seating not less than twenty,

steaming upriver, the reed plumes
whitening at dawn. Motionless, the current
slides, duckweed debris spinning

in a long room with a ceiling fan and wooden
shutters, a veranda with anthuriums
in milk tins, a treadle Singer humming,

in the black eddies. The river coils
back on itself. A hippo surfaces,
yawning like a piano. Acres of lilies undulate

at the head of a flamingo estuary,
with some land like her mother's rice farm
somewhere. Thirty years on her loveliness

as the barge blunders on sunrise, a dugout
on the gold inlet, a net swirls and is cast,
while over their water pots, giggling women

no longer blank, she is flawed with beauty.
Such things are hardly to be written of
– like the offering of beer and maize flour,

semaphore to the bargemen their satiric
invitations, as she turns the page, prettily
incensed by Darcy's too proud proposal.

the pumpkin leaves with coconut, she
pledges in this foreign corner, hallowing
in her mother's name, this plot before she builds.

Oldest Inhabitant

Take the case of Ibne Mucana al-Isbuni,
magistrate, courtier, and Iberian humanist
('*a glass of good wine sets you up for
Friday's prayers*'). He served in Seville
at the court of the Abbadides, and afterwards
with the Zirides in Granada. So fashioned
were his tropes ('*Regard us well, lord,
for our brilliance is to burnish your light,
that light which descends from the Lord
of Creation*') Prince Idris ordered the veil
withdrawn to gaze on the poet's face.

We meet him, sickle in hand, extemporising
satires on the barren soil of the village
of his birth ('*and if the corn exceeds
twenty bags, armies of wild boars descend
from the wilderness of Sintra mountain*').
He has abandoned processing with kings
in their finery to harvest thorns, but his thoughts
are of freedom ('*A man of purpose needs
a windmill, turning with the clouds*').
At this nine centuries' distance, and more,
it seems a rounded life, the journey up

and outwards, the peak, the homecoming
to a known place, a familiar calendar, where
the year begins with the swallows' flight.

Windfall oranges roll among hoop-petticoat
daffodils, and each April brings drought
and the husbanding of water. So much
is evidence. For the rest, from the north
iron-clad Christians, from the Sahara
fundamentalists marched. The complete
poet, the courtier-peasant of my imaginings
vanished, save his metaphors and sickle.

Water

This long summer with the oily tips
of lemon trees curling like copper shavings,
I'm getting to know our *poço*

well. As the valley turns sepia,
and olive trees sharpen their knives,
and the blue gums are shoals of silver fish,

I draw on its quick secrets. At noon,
the shutter thrown back, sunlight
arrows down the green whitewash

to a shimmering, infinitely
beckoning circle and beyond
to water snake flashes in an abyss

impossible to climb from.
Subsisting attuned to a well,
watching the trees breathe, drinking

in birdsong's a throwback
to develop, so
picture me, with my native off-spin,

bowling a plastic bucket to shatter
my face framed in the mirrored
hatch and haul miracle

draughts earth-wards, well
aware if it doesn't flow,
I'm not working hard enough.

Sunday Worship

"This casket India's glowing gems unlocks,
        And all Arabia breathes from yonder box"

The hypermarket has an in-turnstile
with cameras and uniformed guards,
and fifty-six exits, leant on
by the bustling blouses of fifty-six tills.

A coin secures your trolley and you're off
in a boxed maze, rambling as a golf course
and as planned. How's your handicap?
Does your consumer resistance stand up

to ambushes laid by Balmoral Tea (one
pinch per bag per packet in monogrammed
boxes in cellophane wraps), or Formula One
Aftershave, or Mayfair Shower Foam,

or Sheba Coffee, (cinnamon-roast,
with a rubber-nippled Ruandan
doll in a turban), or Tropic of Cancer
Filtertips, or tandoori-flavoured condoms,

or Fatcat Petfood, or Phil A-Tyo lipstick
(the arousing kiss of slaughtered whales),
or the sweatshop colours of Indonesia,
or extra-Virgin-of-Fatima Oils?

Questions not to be asked. What if
the earth turned on its axis, and you
were banana growers for United Fruits,
or quota fishermen burning your boats,

or tea-pickers in their drab lines
where a day's wage's less than a loaf,
and a night's dormitory's for twelve,
and your children will be serfs in turn?

If you're reading this page, the chances
are: most of what you eat,
and much of what you wear,
feeds off another world out there.

They swell, these temples of gluttony,
they encircle our once market towns.
They bring the world to our by-pass,
and they make us serfs in our turn

to the carve-up merchants who own them
and the appetites out of control,
in our search for a meaning to labour,
in the adverts which measure our souls,

while ancient water courses spring,
and the miracle of speech remains,
and childbirth's the joy it always was,
and the hottest day can't wilt the vines,

and each four weeks the full moon,
a yard or two along the horizon,
questions: where in the world
are you going? You're on your own.

Praise Poem

I write in praise of the concrete mixer,
our rotating cuckoo with the fixed yawn.

He swallows sand, he devours gravel
with a bucket of tepid water as chaser.

A cocktail of anatriptic acids
is grist to his iron mill. He spews

grey vomit to spread on our land, and Lo!
earthquake-proof pillars sprout,

sky-scraping in ambition. From his guts
you could out-build the Tower of Babel,

concretising Chomsky's vision
of many tongues, but one deep structure.

In time, his belly will recreate
that bland, pre-lapsarian state

when earth was as smooth as a billiard ball
before Adam's sin released us all

to cracks, gullies, craters, drifts,
fjords, chines, gorges, cliffs,

the Andes and the Himalayas,
the Grand Canyon and San Andreas,

bringing these couplings to a halt
with the celebration of a fault

no concrete mixer will repair:
the fig leaf tangled in Eve's hair.

A Far Cry

The dawn telephone call's
like a wartime telegram
An exchange invites us
to take a call, a voice
swaps distant pleasantries
before the news that dawn
alarm, that brrr-brrr
told of, impacts.

From Africa, these days,
there is only one
unnamed illness. Malaria
or TB, even the customary
Mercedes pile up, we'd
heave a sigh of relief

but this, the doctors
are said not to know,

is the no-hope diagnosis of what
no one dies of until
they've died. So we wait,
aware but not knowing,
wanting to protest but
knowing protest
futile, knowing

Zambia a hecatomb,
Malawi a necropolis,
Mozambique a charnel-
house, from which our
dawn brrr-brrr
announces yet another
friend, cousin,
brother .....

Neighbours

Amadeu, on a plot no bigger than ours,
plants turnips in autumn and potatoes in spring.
He has geese, poultry, two cows and a goat,
with lemon and orange trees, a walnut and hazel,
pumpkins, a turquoise patch of cabbages,
and some carp in a tank fed by our watercourse.
On these riches, which he and his barrel-shaped wife
survey daily in stately perambulation, they
seem to prosper (though it leaves me wondering
who the devil he deals with for his bread and wine?)

Maria António, he of the lead-lined stomach
uncorroded by whatever drip-feeds our well,
owns the forest and a road-side allotment.
The forest's off-limits for planting. He forages
firewood, chestnuts, the odd rabbit or pigeon
with mushrooms and bay for the hunter's pot.
His allotment's resource is the moulded clay
for the miniature windmills with calico sails
he markets to passing tourists. Entrepreneur,
he knows his value, and that of his kind, as decor.

Of the three, Anastásio most resembles us.
He has a van and descends unpredictably
with a kit like a diver's lungs, and insecto-
fungicide for his acre of vines. "The silkworms
and quails take most", he grumbles (or so
says my dictionary for what's more mundane).
But he does it from yearning, having another
life, other manoeuvres for securing his petrol,
his poisons, his satisfactions and his crust. It
makes us accomplices. He's the one I mistrust.

The Platform

John's 19th birthday barbecue
the week before they both depart.
The platform by the old plum tree
that once hurled me to the ground's
yet to be tiled, but no matter.
There's the sound of running water
and a concrete base for tables and chairs,
the charcoal's already tinkling,
and for the first time we can see the spot
Alice chose gets the last of the sunset.

'Haven't you got a light down here?'
says Francisco, protesting the obvious.
By the time the spare ribs are done
it's starlight, and the peppered chicken's
served blindfold but delicious.
There's a good wine and cold beer,
we huddle in the slight chill,
and Alex indulges to the full
his drinking half and opening another,
as we toast John and celebrate his brother.

The looming wall of invisible canna's
a jagged tear at the sky's edge,
to the west, pines are silhouetted,
and revolving above us, in this
breeze from the furrowed Atlantic,
this out-of-town blackness, are
Orion and the Great Bear,
the Plough and distant Pleiades,
conspiring with the hour hand
that returns our sons to England.

I confide to Alice, 'We create
the stage on which they play out
their departures, nothing more.'
But for her, land, ancestors
and inheritance are not oases
on a desert journey, but
the beginning and purposed end.
Each shared meal, every heeled-in
root is like the northern star: a lantern,
a fixity, a magnet, and a legend.

I remember the exodus and the psalms,
the antipodes of my childhood:
the straight and narrow pilgrimage,
the annual round of milk and honey.
Like it or not, they are on their way
and their visits will be seasonal,
Christmas, and familial summer,
as the other loyalties we pray
will be theirs exert their tidal pull,
delivering other ceremonies of survival.

Before the Oranges have Fallen

Bonfire, good fire (Johnson, 1755),
not hell's torment, nor the Inquisition's
auto-da-fé, nor England's yearly

carbonisation of Guy, but benign,
necessary flames. Prune, and burn
before planting, ash for the soil

and pleasure for the soul. On a crisp
afternoon, with an Atlantic view,
and a robin inspecting sawn-off

lichens, as my smoke's shadow
purples the up-turned earth,
I am feeding a fire, with plum

and apple prunings. This
isn't Tyger, nor Hopkins' forge,
nor Eliot's dove with the flickering

tongue descending in damnation,
nor am I priest nor presbyter
consummating the millennium, just

a man greying with average wisdom,
glad that spring comes early here
before the oranges have fallen,

ignorant of any need to make
poetry of the fact I love
lighting and tending a bon fire.

Shepherd

Accelerating on the Sintra Road,
overtaking to beat the lights,
I was astonished by a shepherd
on a hillock, off to the right.

It was opposite the golf course,
where the advert for *Villas Byron*
says, *Come and live close
to Nature* in a fenced condominium.

These lines being unreflective,
I drove on past the prison shop,
the schools, American and Convent,
the roundabout where I didn't stop,

off down the Lisbon slip road, and
back to Trajouce and Carrascal,
that Euro-industrial wasteland
where labour's cheap, and illegal.

All of this, he'd been staring
at, great PAN on his mound,
with his staff, and his scavenging
black sheep, out of bounds.

Dry Stone Walls

Two channel streams, the third secures
the two-metre precipice to the forest.
Boundaries. When a stone here
before the language I use existed is
dislodged, it's mere custom to replace it.

There's rhythm in dry stone walls,
mineral shifts from crystal to ochre,
to turquoise and scarlet in the toe-hold
plantlings, the mosses and lichens,
each minute and back from sunlight to cloud.

Yet thistledown invades and bees plunder
unprosecuted. Our snake ignores
the watercourse boulders that suck
its bootlace in, and swallows
are untrammelled in their private creole

of clicks and screams. I love old walls,
I admire wall breachers. I condemn
new walls. I thrive on privacy.
There's no resolving this conundrum
as the sound of water sculpting stones

blends with the piping of hatched
martins, a blessing on our eaves.
All histories, all beliefs take off
somewhere from this image, building
their subtle, self-validating systems.

It all turns on the four elements:
shelter, partnership, offspring,
and the possibilities of story. Within
these walls, there's living to be done.
After the house, there's still the travelling on.

Mightier than, etc

For Senhor João Fonseca Gil Vincent,
his bulldozer's a precision instrument.

He could smash that 200 year olive bole
with a single uppercut, and does the inevitable,

but he prefers a featherlite dusting, a neat
filleting of culverts and driveways, that

depends on exact poise, viz., four
pile-driving telescopes opening at singular

angles to calibrated levels
(the millstone tyres revolving

uselessly) so the contraption rears
like a monster cockroach, and our senhor

with his gap-toothed digger
and a battery of levers

pats and smoothes and nudges and prods
his boulders and clods

as though icing a cake,
or planting a mosaic,

or crafting a more elegant lyric
than these elephant-foot iambics,

- for as he watches the writer
watching the constructor

there's detectable irony
in his reined-in delicacy.

The mightier pen,
the sword into ploughshare,

hardly seem options
when it's ballpoint and bulldozer.

With What I'm Burning

Two years on I know
these logs, from the tree
to the woodpile to our
December hearth. Sweet
apple and damson, the ivy-
strangled olive branch,
the peach bough torn
by weight of fruit, and that
invading cork-oak, with its
pulpy bark and heart
of ebony, all familiar
to the very saw cut
and verdigris coins of lichen.

A late-born sensation
this, to know how/where with what
I'm burning grew, something
seasoned, like grief.

Victor

The poem wrote itself. The unbearably
tender youth smiling up
from the hospital bed at the impossibly
lovely sisters bending over him
all their curves and concern, and at

the edge of the frame the iron-faced
white man, with rimless
spectacles and jaw like a clamp,
staring over the photographer's
right shoulder. But the picture deceives.

This was no prison warder or PIDE
goon, but a loving
father repressing tears of fury
at his brown son's dismembering
in a war he never credited (and was

lost, and is long forgotten). Today
Victor shows us this,
among pictures of him whole. Then
exhibits his technology. A right leg
with its circuitry. A right arm

with a built-in brain, responsive
to his own. There's
laughter as he swivels his hand
360°. But he won't pick up
his wineglass, lest the eight kilo

robocop grip crush it to smithereens.

Literary Remains

Vasco's used to the latest custom,
but his father was appalled when
between the lying-in and the funeral
the corpse was abandoned overnight.

'Overnight? In England, it's frozen
in the morgue till the family
drifts in from wherever with time
off work, maybe ten days or more.'

Now it's Vasco's scandalised. But he
has a grim duty. Here, the buried enjoy
a five year tenure before the bones
are lifted and boxed in the vault,

this resurrection needing a family
member present in law to approve
- his aunt, for instance, so embalmed
by her pills she took seven years

to qualify for the skeleton cupboard.
Babies, says Vasco, disturb him most
with their tiny rosaries and bird-like
ribs, and I yield him the palm

in this tournament of the macabre,
he being half my age in a matter ever
closer to the bone, and I far from re-
hearsed in my curtain-line rattle.

The Double Wake

Four months the skies have wept
unceasingly, but today she's back
hoeing again where once were flowerbeds,

her mourning, after this winter's
second bereavement and as close
to the heart strings, calmer. Twice

were things to be done, not just dogs
going on with their doggy life, but life
for the participants, tickets

to be bought, clothes ironed, a coffin
ordered, airports to be faced
where everything you have to do's

a denial of all you're feeling. Then
the vacuity of flight. By the time
there's time for grief, there's already

the desolation of grief somehow missed,
that sitting all night with the newly dead
that delivers them their due. But after

this rain-swept winter when the skies
have loured like Adamastor of the Storms,
the sluiced flowerbeds are stirring

with tubers she had forgotten, crocuses,
ammonites and grape hyacinths,
and before the oranges have fallen,

the almond trees are in tiny leaf.
She's back, communing in the cold
sunlight of the year's turn, in that patch

cleared of ironical balm - more real
than any words of mine who'd
juggle planets to lighten her double grief.

An Open Letter to Derek Walcott

We met three times, though hardly to your
recalling, the buzz being all mine
in a sorry case of poet worship, you

UWI guest lecturer, fingering the obligatory
academic funerary, muttering
'does this stuff come off?' before

your spiel about Buñuel's *Crusoe*, you
war-flecked, scene-painting
for Soyinka's *The Road*, demanding

I cross my heart to buy tickets, you
wandering on the TV set of an evangelical
show I'd set my steelband to (for

their sponsor's sake), and absconding
in disgust. Not the right ambience, though
our former wives had tea once,

apparently through us. From your *Green Night*
onwards, I've shadowed your theme
of the ends of empire, though with

nowhere, despite these triplets, to be *Castaway*
to, each continental voyage confirming
my UK-ness, laureate of our post-

colonial sleepwalk, and envying your
freedom from the imperial mark
of Cain to name with love and a deeper

possession, your people and their places.
Your *Gulf* confirmed our separation, sailing
off with your rightful inheritance, this

English language re-coined with Elizabethan
boldness, while I was left picking over
what could be accurately said, given

what I had seen, in strict fairness, as heir
to a four-hundred-year lie. Where you
named, I followed like a dictionary

defining. When reviewers called
my *Bounty* a 'balladic counterpoint
to your *Omerus*', I was

beside myself with promotion, till
masterly you assumed theme and title
and made them wholly your own.

Yet like the F.O. librarian once
encountered in Whitehall, who bewailed
that with the empowerment

of each released agitator, another
bookcase crossed the yard
to the swish Commonwealth suite, I have

territory to defend: *Stedman*, who
found in the swamp forest
himself as husband and lover, conserving

a style in the *Stockade* I'd no option
but to write back from, even as
the maroons became his heroes, choosing

a *South* where poetry flows
too deep for executive decisions,
making happen what's endlessly

beyond resolution, while scorning
superfluity like the *Traveller's
Palm*'s green fountain. I've

unearthed in your exuberant shadow
matter you don't write about:
the harrowed, punctilious

extravagance of those who are still in charge.

Roman Style

The scythe's discarded blade with its gap tooth
rusts on the veranda. Spring's flowers
are levelled, the field lies bare

to contours the swallows shave unerringly.
Our feeling's of summer no sooner come
than gone, but l never cease marvelling

about the seasons here, how harvest's
but a prelude to Julho and Agosto,
Roman inserted months, when the sun

scours like a blow torch, and our resort's
once more to our well-spring. It's not
what we are at heart feels different,

perhaps a little heavier, somewhat
slower to the beach ball, while judges,
presidents, even golfers, are ever younger,

and no TV adverts target us in their mooning
mock-Hollywood, thank god, for jeans
or face creams or exercise contraptions

as friends are crossing into the dark,
and it touches family ever closer. So,
the hatch sealed, we've sized up the well

with a pump buoy, and regale nightly
all we've planted with more than ever
loving and lavish draughts, hoping

Roman-fashion to insure against
something when the scythe rounds
on its owner and the plot lies bare.

The Exploding Gorse-Pods

Our friends come out from the city
to our picnic platform with their delightful
son, just walking, just beginning to talk
and so enveloped with love he looks
outward smiling, and the world's

his for the making as we learn Senegal's
won improbably, and the meal's
a summer lasagne, and the wine's a smokey
Trincadeira, and the new government's
tax plans are worse than unjust they're

incompetent, and all he has to do is chuckle
or pick up the tiniest pebble and bring us,
and all our concerns are nothing to this
outward-looking baby whose four
words have us all repeating them, and gurgles

his approval. Little dictator, you have us
by the heart-strings. You turn our projects
upside down. You're like the finches
shrilling from the pine trees now
the new kernels are ripe for dispersal,

or the marigolds blazing, or thistle-
heads seeding, or the exploding gorse-
pods your parents have come out here for
to refresh themselves and replenish
us, but more. Incomparably more.

As Goldfinches are Stabbing the First Green Cones

There are plants, for example, so whole-hearted
in their being, you don't need to wait
for their fruits to attest them.

Lemon trees are lemony to the tips of their newest
mahogany buds, no mistaking a lemon for a mere grapefruit,
or toning its acids down with goat manure,

and basil, just stroll past it, and the whirl of air's
enough to permeate the whole walk way,
or eucalyptus, best after a shower,

with its silver-fish foliage and rolled–plasticine bark,
the merest sun-dried sliver of which
radiates its camphor. Alice broils

pumpkin leaves with the yellow flowers and a speckled
globe, the milky chlorophyll pulsing throughout.
Or take pine trees this July evening as

goldfinches are stabbing the first green cones, just
scratch the trunk, and the weeping's pure pine.
Then there's walnuts with their dedication

to silverplate bark and silver green foliage
and their incorruptible nose-cone hardness.
As for vines, already their leaves are predicting

October's purple and white musts. It's how I
was taught, and I still reckon, a poem should be
to the least comma

(though, of course, there's also much to be said for lying).

The Two Markers

Having travelled, perhaps, too much of the world
to learn much about it, I've abandoned
hunting and gathering for a garden
with not much by way of autumn colour,

the cork oaks being dark as ever, just
rather more leathery, the olives as silver-grey,
while the poplars shed their leaves
without troubling about seasonal show, as

well into November, long after the swallows'
departure, and the tramping of the grapes,
there are warm bright days, and with these rains
the illusion of springtime and planting.

But there are two markers, these yellow
afternoons with their early dusk, to gratify
with a proper sense of where I'm at:
a patch of Periquita vines, between

the picking and the pruning, like an Afghan
carpet in its three-dimensional reds: and
an avenue of plane trees, winding away
from the locked wrought-iron gates, in ever-

receding liturgical purple and gold. I
embrace and continue wondering, in charity
with the road. May my autumn, tolerant
poems find fit audience, and be fertile.

When Paul Celan Met Heidegger

When Paul Celan met Heidegger
in that Black Forest hut

where the philosopher and nature met
in the manner of soiled centuries,

his question hung in the damp air:
what of Jews and the Gypsies?

Blue-eyed Hitler, vegecologist,
anti-smoker and folklorist,

concentrated all wanderers
and earthed them in his fires.

Such was the poet's right to ask
the philosopher was silenced,

and it echoes whenever a plot's
patrolled, viz., what

of refugees, aliens,
asylum-seekers, Palestinians?

Celan found beautiful sport in the orchid.
I write in praise of the canine hybrid

that claims its space by hoisting
a leg, no matter who planted the lamppost.

Index of Titles

Index of First Lines